**FREIGHT
BOOKS**

VERSschmuggel

Gedichte: deutsch, englisch, schottisch-gälisch

RYAN VAN WINKLE

PETER MACKAY

ANNA CROWE

ROBIN ROBERTSON

J. O. MORGAN

DON PATERSON

Herausgegeben von
Edited by

Ein Projekt der
A project by

Wunderhorn

reVERSible

Poems: german, english, scottish-gaelic

BJÖRN KUHLIGK

DAGMARA KRAUS

ODILE KENNEL

ULRIKE DRAESNER

KATHARINA SCHULTENS

MICHAEL DONHAUSER

Thomas Wohlfahrt
Aurélie Maurin

Literaturwerkstatt
Berlin

Freight

8 Foreword   Vorwort 9

RYAN VAN WINKLE   **BJÖRN KUHLIGK**
16 The Apartment   Die Wohnung 17
20 Babel   Babel 21
22 Untitled   Ohne Titel 23
24 My 100-Year-Old Ghost   Mein 100 Jahre alter Geist 25

BJÖRN KUHLIGK   RYAN VAN WINKLE
Das Gedicht geht durch einen   The poem travels through a body
30 Körper und grüßt nicht mal – 1   and doesn't even nod hello – I 31
32 2   I I 33
34 3   I I I 35
36 4   IV 37
38 5   V 39
40 6   VI 41

PETER MACKAY   DAGMARA KRAUS
46 New World   Aus der neuen Welt 47
48 In Cordoba / Ann an Cordoba   In Córdoba 49
50 In the British Museum /
50 Ann an Ard-Mhuseaum Bhreatainn   Im British Museum 51
52 When I think of the incommunicable /
Nuair a smaoineachas mi air   Wenn ich an das
52 na tha do-thuigsinneach   Unvermittelbare denke 53
54 The Leak / An t-Aoidean   Das Leck 55

DAGMARA KRAUS   PETER MACKAY
58 nur mut, mond   Be brave, moon 59
60 fatrasien 1   Fantrasies 1 61
62 fatrasien 2   Fantrasies 2 63
64 fatrasien 3   Fantrasies 3 65
66 triskele   Triskelion 67

ANNA CROWE　　　　　ODILE KENNEL
74　A Calendar of Hares　　Hasenkalender　75
78　A Shepherd's voice　　Stimme eines Schäfers　79
80　Mended fence, Barra　　Geflickter Zaun auf Barra　81
84　Sari　　　　　　　　　Sari　85

ODILE KENNEL　　　　　ANNA CROWE
wenn ich die Augen schließe,　when I close my eyes
90　ist der Himmel ein Bagger　the sky is a digger　91
92　im Hof der tschatschenden Frisöre　in the chatching hairdressers' backyard　93
96　Tiere zu fragen　　　bestial questions　97
98　nach Pasárgada　　　going to Pasárgada　99
100　die metaphorische Logik einer Verbindung　the metaphorical logic of a connection　101

ROBIN ROBERTSON　　　ULRIKE DRAESNER
106　Annunciation　　　Verkündigung　107
108　The Fishermen's Farewell　Die Ausfahrt der Fischer　109
110　The Shelter　　　Obdach　111
112　Glass of Water and Coffee Pot　Wasserglas mit Kaffeekanne　113

ULRIKE DRAESNER　　　ROBIN ROBERTSON
116　chlorophyll　　　Chlorophyll　117
118　schöneweide, schöneweide　Schöneweide, Schöneweide　119

J. O. MORGAN　　　　KATHARINA SCHULTENS
130　Take two small goats　nimm zwei junge Ziegen　131
132　It's akin to a Venn diagram　eventuell: ein Diagramm　133
134　The shelves may be lined　in den Regalen Buch um Buch　135
136　Long after check out time　die Checkoutzeit ist längst vorbei　137
138　'Who kissed me?'　　»Wer hat mich geküsst?«　139

KATHARINA SCHULTENS　J. O. MORGAN
144　Prism　　　　　Prism　145
146　hidden liquidity　　Hidden Liquidity　147
148　hysteresis　　　Hysteresis　149
152　bärenmarkt　　　Bear Market　153
156　dark pools　　　Dark Pools　157

DON PATERSON   MICHAEL DONHAUSER

162 Wave   Welle 163
164 A Vow   Ein Schwur 165
166 Apsinthion   Apsinthion 167
168 The Big Listener   Der große Zuhörer 169
170 Francesca Woodman   Francesca Woodman 171

MICHAEL DONHAUSER   DON PATERSON

174 Vielleicht an einem Abend   Late perhaps one evening 175
176 Aber wir werden   Through the night 177
178 Es war   It was 179
180 Vielleicht   Maybe 181
182 Die Platanen   Take the maples 183
184 Regnet es   Did it rain 185
186 Es gab, da war der Mond   There was – then the moon 187
188 Bitter sei und so blieb   They say it was harsh 189
190 Wie der Wind streifte   O how the wind brushed 191

194 BIOGRAPHIES   BIOGRAPHIEN 195
206 HERAUSGEBER   EDITORS 206
207 URHEBERRECHTLICHE HINWEISE   COPYRIGHT INFORMATIONS 207

INTERLINEARÜBERSETZUNGEN	INTERLINEAR TRANSLATIONS
Clara Sondermann	(Ryan Van Winkle und J. O. Morgan)
Donna Stonecipher	(Björn Kuhligk)
Charlotte Thiessen / Sam Langer	(Peter Mackay)
Joseph Given	(Dagmara Kraus)
Charlotte Thiessen / Joel Scott	(Anna Crowe)
Katy Derbyshire	(Odile Kennel)
Tom Morrison	(Ulrike Draesner)
Joseph Given	(Katharina Schultens)
Charlotte Thiessen / Sam Langer	(Don Paterson)
Donal McLaughlin	(Michael Donhauser)

FOREWORD

Scottish poetry is an insider tip for German poets, and the other way around; there has been little translation or publication activity between the two. For us Germans, the charm of Scottish poetry lies in its long, grand tradition, and in the poetic quality of Gaelic which this poetry transports as melodic and narrative knowledge even when written in English. This is joined by our notion of the archaic splendour of the Scottish landscape which suffuses this very modern poetry.

And for Scottish readers?

In his poem "Das Gedicht geht durch einen Körper und grüsst nicht mal", Björn Kuhligk writes: "Rede ich über Gedichte, denke ich, ich sollte nicht darüber reden". Ryan van Winkle's translation is terser: If I talk about poems, I shouldn't be talking. Nonetheless, the poets in this anthology spent days talking, laughing and pondering poetry. Their conversations revolved around nuclear physics and animal slaughter, astrology, mythology and the black magic of the financial markets. On their shared journey through these two worlds of language and thought, the authors found that none of them knew, for instance, whether cottage cheese is made of cow's or goat's milk, or whether the arms of a starfish can grow back.

Ultimately this volume brings together poems that have been smuggled back and forth across language borders until the result was good poetry in a new language. Every single poem is a 3D-installation of sound and rhythm, a game with the possibilities of language and its intended meaning. All that must be translated. It was translated successfully because in each case the original poet, a colleague, was able to grant the freedoms essential to the translation process.

What exactly took place?

Invited by the Literaturwerkstatt Berlin, six Scottish and six German poets met at the *poesiefestival berlin* 2014 for the translation workshop "reVERSible", taking on the adventure of translating one another without necessarily understanding each other's language. Though this may sound absurd at first, it is based on a sophisticated method and guarantees ideal translations.

VORWORT

Schottische Dichtung und deutsche Gedichte sind ein Geheimtipp füreinander, zumal sie per Übersetzung und verlegerisch betreut kaum zugänglich sind. Für uns deutschsprachige Leser liegt der Reiz sicher in der großen und langen Tradition, über welche die schottische Dichtung verfügt, sowie in der Poetizität des Gälischen, die diese Dichtung, auch dann, wenn sie englisch verfasst ist, als klangliches wie narratives Wissen mitführt. Hinzu kommt sicher die von uns als archaisch und prächtig wahrgenommene Landschaft Schottlands, aus der heraus sich diese sehr moderne Dichtung auch speist.

Und für die schottisch-englischen Leser?

In seinem Poem »das Gedicht geht durch einen Körper und grüßt nicht mal« schreibt Björn Kuhligk: Rede ich über Gedichte, denke ich, ich sollte nicht darüber reden. Ryan van Winkles Übersetzung ist knapper: If I talk about poems, I shouldn't be talking. Nichtsdestotrotz haben die Dichter dieser Anthologie tagelang gemeinsam über Gedichte geredet, gelacht und gegrübelt. Die Gespräche drehten sich um Kernphysik und Tierschlachtung, Astrologie, Mythologie und die schwarze Magie der Finanzmärkte. Auf der gemeinsamen Reise durch die beiden Sprach- und Denkwelten stellten die Autoren fest, dass letztlich niemand von ihnen wusste, ob Hüttenkäse aus Kuh- oder Ziegenmilch hergestellt wird, oder ob die Arme des Seesterns nachwachsen können.

Letztendlich aber vereint dieser Band Gedichte, die über Sprachgrenzen so lange hin und her geschmuggelt wurden, bis sie in der neuen Sprache wieder ein gutes Gedicht ergaben. Denn: Ein jedes Gedicht ist eine 3D-Installation aus Klang und Rhythmus, dem Spiel mit den Möglichkeiten von Sprache und dem, was das Gedicht bedeuten will. All das musste übersetzt werden. Es gelang, weil die notwendigen Freiheiten, die dem Übersetzungsprozess unabdingbar sind, vom Dichter des Originals, der Kollege war, gewährt werden konnten.

Wie war das möglich?

Auf Einladung der Literaturwerkstatt Berlin trafen sich im Rahmen des *poesiefestival berlin* 2014 sechs schottische und sechs deutschsprachige DichterInnen in Berlin, um im Übersetzungsworkshop »VERSschmuggel«

AURÉLIE MAURIN | THOMAS WOHLFAHRT

The poets work in pairs on the basis of pre-produced gloss translations, which indicate a range of language possibilities and open up paths for the actual translation process. Each pair is facilitated by an interpreter who ensures that both poets can communicate in their native languages as they tell their translating colleagues the stories behind the poems, precisely, intensely and very personally. The 3D-installation of the poem comes to life, revealing its dimensions. All this must now be transformed into the target language, or rather reinvented there.

Thus a direct dialogue develops, an intensive, individual smuggling of stylistic interconnections, cultural connotations, poetic traditions and compositional methods. The result is translations of the highest quality, aftersongs.

This bilingual volume pairs originals with their translations. Readers can reconstruct the decisions which the poets made in order to allow the poems to take form anew in a foreign language. The poems and their translations are joined by short essays written by the participating poets, which offer glimpses into each poetic workshop and capture an echo of the translation act itself.

QR codes make it technologically possible to hear the instrument of the poem, the human voice. While reading the book, readers can simultaneously hear the poems read by the poets themselves. It will be interesting to see how, for instance, commuters will read this poetry collection with their ear glued to their smartphone in order to capture the auditory dimension. The links also offer audible proof that translation is not a rule-bound process tied to grammar and dictionaries, but rather a constant act of interpretation. In each constellation, the poets have brought their own poetological tone into the translation.

We wish all our readers and listeners the greatest of pleasure on this expedition into the depths of linguistic and poetic worlds. We wish to extend our heartfelt thanks to all the translators of the glosses, without whose skills none of this would have been possible. We also thank all those who were involved in a direct or advisory fashion in the realization of this unique project, especially Robyn Marsack of the Scottish Poetry Library, Marijke Brouwer of the British Council, Michael Mechner for conducting and producing the sound recordings, and Charlotte Thiessen for her assistance in the implementation of the entire project.

das Abenteuer zu wagen, sich gegenseitig zu übersetzen, ohne die Sprache des anderen notwendig zu verstehen. Was zunächst absurd klingen mag, beruht auf einem methodischen Konzept und garantiert beste Übertragungen in die jeweils andere Sprache.

Die DichterInnen arbeiteten paarweise mit vorab angefertigten Interlinearübersetzungen als Grundlage. Diese wiesen eine Aneinanderreihung von sprachlichen Möglichkeiten auf und eröffneten den Weg zum eigentlichen Übersetzen. Zwischen jedem Paar agierte ein Sprachmittler und sorgte dafür, dass beide Dichter in ihren Muttersprachen bleiben und ihrem übersetzenden Dichterkollegen die Geschichten erzählen konnten, die hinter den Gedichten liegen; sehr genau, sehr intensiv, sehr persönlich. Die 3D-Installation Gedicht wurde lebendig und offenbarte ihre Dimensionen. Dies alles galt es nun, in die Zielsprache zu transformieren bzw. dort neu zu erfinden.

So entstand ein direkter Austausch, der ein intensives und individuelles Schmuggeln von stilistischen Zusammenhängen, kulturellen Konnotationen, poetischen Traditionen und Kompositionsverfahren ermöglichte. Entstanden sind Nachdichtungen vom Feinsten, aftersongs.

Der vorliegende zweisprachige Band vereint Original und Übersetzung. Der Leser kann bei der Lektüre nachvollziehen, welche Entscheidungen die Dichter getroffen haben, um das eigene Gedicht in der jeweils anderen Sprache wieder erstehen zu lassen. Ergänzt werden die Gedichte und deren Übersetzungen durch kurze Essays, die von den beteiligten Dichtern verfasst wurden und einen Einblick in die jeweilige Dichter-Werkstatt gewähren sowie einen Widerhall vom Übersetzungsakt selbst geben.

QR-Codes machen es technisch möglich, das Instrument des Gedichts, die menschliche Stimme, zu hören. Der Leser ist in der Lage, beim Lesen des Bandes mitzuhören, wie es klingt, wenn das Gedicht vom Dichter selbst gelesen wird. Zukünftig werden also zum Beispiel Bahnfahrende beim Lesen dieser Gedichtsammlung mit dem Telefon am Ohr der klanglichen Dimension der Texte lauschen können. Die Links machen zudem hörbar, dass Übersetzen kein strenger, der Grammatik und dem Wörterbuch gehorchender Vorgang ist, sondern ein stetes Interpretieren. In jeder Konstellation haben die Dichter ihren jeweils eigenen poetologischen Ton in die Übersetzung mit eingebracht.

The translator Tom Morrison, whose charm, wit and professionalism brightened the atmosphere of the entire group, will remain in our thoughts. He passed away just a few weeks after the workshop. This anthology is dedicated to him.

Berlin, September 2015

Allen Lesern und Hörern wünschen wir viel Vergnügen bei dieser Expedition in die Tiefen sprachlicher und poetischer Welten. Wir möchten uns sehr herzlich bei allen ÜbersetzerInnen der Interlinearversion bedanken, ohne deren Kompetenz nichts hätte gelingen können. Ebenso danken wir allen, die beratend oder unmittelbar an der Realisierung dieses einzigartigen Projekts mitgewirkt haben, insbesondere Robyn Marsack von der Scottish Poetry Library, Marijke Brouwer vom British Council, Michael Mechner für die Tonaufnahmen und deren Bearbeitung sowie Charlotte Thiessen für ihre Mitwirkung bei der Durchführung des gesamten Projektes.

Unsere Gedanken gelten dem Übersetzer Tim Morrison, dessen Charme, Witz und Professionalität für gute Laune in der gesamten Gruppe sorgten. Nur wenige Wochen nach dem Workshop ist er verstorben. Diese Anthologie sei ihm gewidmet.

Berlin, September 2015

RYAN VAN WINKLE }

interpreter }
Sprachmittlerin }

{ BJÖRN KUHLIGK

{ Donna Stonecipher

THE APARTMENT

Our new walls,
empty in the dusk,
hang like sheets
before first light.

There is a driven nail
by the stove that could
hold a pan if the walls
stay sturdy. And the

old tenants left a mirror in the
bedroom which looks back
at staring walls with fine cracks
like a museum's basement vase

there are brown smears
in the study – chocolate, blood
or shit, we don't know what
will happen to us here or what

will settle on rented walls
or if nothing will settle
at all. We've just moved

and already we are bitter
cranberries in each other's
mouths, biting about photos,
the place of the table, lay

of the bed. The apartment is a City
Hall we cannot fight. So we turn
like lawyers, against each other,
let the walls stare. There is a mirror

DIE WOHNUNG

Unsere neuen Wände
leer in der Abenddämmerung
hängen wie Laken
vor dem ersten Licht.

Da ist ein eingeschlagener Nagel
neben dem Herd, der könnte
eine Pfanne halten, wenn die Wände
standhaft bleiben. Und die

alten Mieter ließen einen Spiegel im
Schlafzimmer, der zurücksieht auf
die glotzenden Wände mit feinen Rissen
wie auf eine Vase im Museumskeller

es gibt braune Schlieren
im Arbeitszimmer – Schokolade, Blut
oder Scheiße, wir wissen nicht, was
uns hier passieren wird oder was

sich an den gemieteten Wänden ablagern wird
oder ob sich überhaupt etwas
ablagert. Wir sind gerade umgezogen

und schon sind wir bittere
Preiselbeeren im Mund des anderen
streiten uns verbissen wegen Fotos
dem Platz des Tisches, der Position

des Bettes. Die Wohnung ist die Verwaltung
dagegen kommen wir nicht an. Also wenden wir uns
wie Anwälte gegeneinander
lassen die Wände starren. Da ist ein Spiegel

to look into, a nail to hang onto.
Our unopened boxes hide in corners
and closets like beaten children.
And we will take the blood

off the walls and the dust
from the shelves. We have one
year together in a place that
is empty at dusk and feels like fog

inside and between us,
and Christ, tomorrow,
we will live here.

zum Reinsehen, ein Nagel zum Dranhängen.
Unsere ungeöffneten Kartons verstecken sich in Ecken
und Schränken wie verprügelte Kinder.
Und wir werden das Blut von den Wänden

wischen und den Staub
von den Regalen. Wir sind nun für ein
Jahr zusammen an einem Ort, der
leer ist in der Abenddämmerung und sich anfühlt wie Grauschleier

in und zwischen uns,
und Herrgott, morgen
werden wir hier leben.

BABEL

Our good sex was building
a Babel. We were fucking
our way up the tower
and God saw us coming.
And so there came
months we could not
fuck. We remembered
the tower as it was written:
The people God slung
all over the Earth, speaking
incoherent to each other
as we do when you moan
the dishes, say I don't listen.
And when I say you cut
the bread crooked or
over-salt the pasta you hear
my words as Greek and I know
our sex was looked at
and the Lord said: "Look,
they are one people
and they have all one
language; and this is only
the beginning of what
they may do." And so
you come to me at night,
and some nights I come
before you: humble flesh,
with a different tongue.

BABEL

Unser guter Sex errichtete
ein Babel. Wir fickten
uns Schicht um Schicht den Turm hoch
und Gott sah uns kommen.
Und so, so kamen
Monate, in denen wir nicht ficken
konnten. Wir erinnerten uns
an den Turm, wie es geschrieben stand:
Die Menschen warf Gott
überall auf die Erde hin, sie sprachen
miteinander ohne Zusammenhang
wie wir das tun, wenn du stöhnst
das Geschirr, und sagst, ich höre nicht zu.
Und wenn ich sage, du schneidest
das Brot schief oder
versalzst die Nudeln, hörst du
mir zu, als würde ich chinesisch sprechen, und ich weiß
wir wurden beim Sex beobachtet
und der Herr sagte: »Sehet
sie sind ein Volk
und sie haben alle eine
Sprache; und dies ist nur
der Anfang von dem
was sie tun könnten.« Und so
kommst du zu mir bei Nacht
und in manchen Nächten komme ich
vor dir: demütiges Fleisch
die Zunge in anderer Sprache.

UNTITLED

> Nothing can be lost by taking time. If there be an object to hurry any
> of you, in hot haste, to a step you would never take deliberately, that
> object will be frustrated by taking time; but no good object can be
> frustrated by it.
> *Abraham Lincoln*

Time is nothingness
and this should allow
me to take any transport

I want. And I will not
hurry in hot haste nor
will I look to time

as a challenger,
or to you who rushed
to that train

thinking you were late.
The moon was falling,
tripping over your bags,

and I was wanting
to say you were not late,
that the train would come

again and again
like a dream of falling,
like a star

fish regrowing its arms.
And my arms and time
are nothingness and that

should allow you to take
them in your own time,
deliberately, like boarding

a train you know you want,
with a solid name and a destination
stamped on the front in final letters.

OHNE TITEL

> Nichts Wertvolles kann verloren gehen, wenn wir uns Zeit lassen. Wenn es eine
> Absicht gibt, irgendeinem von euch in heißer Hast einen Schritt aufzudrängen,
> den ihr nie bewusst gehen würdet, dann wird diese Absicht vereitelt, indem man
> sich Zeit gönnt; aber keine gute Absicht kann dadurch geschmälert werden.
> *Abraham Lincoln*

Zeit ist Nichts
und das sollte mir erlauben
jedes Verkehrsmittel zu nehmen

das ich will. Und ich werde nicht
hetzen in heißer Hast noch
werde ich die Zeit

als einen Herausforderer betrachten
oder dich, die du
zu diesem Zug ranntest

dachtest, du wärst zu spät.
Der Mond sank
stolperte über deine Koffer

und ich wollte dir die ganze Zeit sagen
dass du nicht zu spät bist
dass der Zug immer wieder

kommen würde
wie ein Falltraum
wie die Arme

eines Seesterns, die wieder nachwachsen.
Und meine Arme und Zeit
sind Nichts und das

sollte dir erlauben, sie
in deine eigene Zeit zu nehmen
bewusst, wie das Einsteigen

in einen Zug, den du unbedingt nehmen willst
der mit einer soliden Bezeichnung und einer Richtung
abgestempelt ist auf der Vorderseite in bleibenden Buchstaben.

MY 100-YEAR-OLD GHOST

sits up with me when the power cuts,
tells about the trout at Unkee's Lake,

the wood house burned on the hill.
He says he was intimate with every

leaf of grass. Wore one hat
for Griswold, another for his own field,

the possibilities of the century laid out;
an endless string of fishing pools. But

they never got ahead of my ghost –
he took them like cows, one at a time,

never lusted for the color of trout
in a pool a mile away.

He knew from the smoke in the sky
Mrs. Johnson was starting supper, and, in March,

when the candles appeared,
he knew Bobby's boy had died.

My ghost only ever had one bar
where the keeper didn't water his drinks,

nor did he feel the need to hide his moth cap,
his potato clothes, or scrub himself birth pink.

My ghost tells me there was a time you'd look out
and not find a Dairy Queen. You could sit

on your porch a whole life and never think
about China. Sometimes I see my ghost

bringing cut sunflowers to his wife
and it seems so simple.

MEIN 100 JAHRE ALTER GEIST

bleibt wach mit mir, wenn der Strom ausfällt
erzählt von den Forellen im Unkee's Lake

dem niedergebrannten Holzhaus auf dem Hügel.
Er sagt, er sei vertraut gewesen mit jedem

Grashalm. Ging er zu Griswold, trug er eine Arbeitshose
auf seinem Feld hatte er seine eigene an

die Möglichkeiten des Jahrhunderts lagen vor ihm:
eine endlose Schnur von Angelteichen. Aber

die Teiche überforderten nie meinen Geist –
er nahm sie wie Kühe, eine nach der anderen

begehrte nie die Farbe der Forellen
in einem anderen Teich.

Er wusste vom Rauch am Himmel
Mrs. Johnson hatte mit dem Abendessen begonnen, und, im März

als die Kerzen plötzlich brannten
wusste er, dass Bobbys Junge gestorben war.

Mein Geist ging immer nur in eine Kneipe
wo der Wirt die Drinks nicht mit Wasser verdünnte

noch fand er es notwendig, seine Mottenmütze zu verstecken
seine Plünnen, oder sich babyrosa zu schrubben.

Mein Geist erzählt mir von der Zeit, in der man aufblicken
und keinen Dairy Queen finden würde. Du konntest

ein ganzes Leben lang auf deinem Vordach sitzen und
niemals an China denken. Manchmal sehe ich meinen Geist

wie er seiner Frau Sonnenblumen für die Vase bringt
und es scheint so einfach.

Then, sometimes, it is dark,
he's just in from work and Griswold says

they ain't going to raise his pay. And even back then
the power went out, long nights when they had no kerosene.

And my ghost tries to sell me on simpler times:
the grass soft, endless –

lampless nights,
pools of crickets singing.

Dann, manchmal, ist es dunkel
er ist gerade zurück von der Arbeit und Griswold sagt

sie werden seinen Lohn nicht erhöhen. Und sogar damals
fiel der Strom aus, lange Nächte, in denen sie kein Petroleum hatten.

Und mein Geist versucht mich für einfachere Zeiten zu gewinnen:
Das Gras sanft, endlos –

Nächte ohne Lampen
Schwärme zirpender Grillen.

BJÖRN KUHLIGK }

interpreter }
Sprachmittlerin }

{ **RYAN VAN WINKLE**

{ Donna Stonecipher

DAS GEDICHT GEHT DURCH EINEN KÖRPER
UND GRÜSST NICHT MAL

1

Wenn man durch ein Land reist, ist das Land eine Reise wert.
Wenn man eine Siedlung verlässt, erreicht man eine andere.
Wenn man ein Gedicht geschrieben hat, schreibt man ein nächstes.
Wenn das eine Freude ist, ist das eine Freude.
Wenn man ein Bier trinkt, trinkt man ein Bier.
Wenn das schön ist, ist es schön.
Wenn ich das so weiter mache, mache ich so weiter damit.
Wenn ich einen Wurstsalat esse, esse ich einen Wurstsalat.
Wenn das eine Freude ist, dann ist das eine Freude.
Wenn man das eigene Leben als Material benutzt, dann ist das so.
Wenn man eine neue Grammatik erfinden möchte, kann man das tun.
Wenn man eine neue Wahrnehmung erzeugen möchte, kann man das tun.
Wenn man etwas zertrümmern möchte, möchte man etwas zertrümmern.
Wenn man etwas tun möchte, möchte man etwas tun.
Wenn man das jetzt so weitermacht, dann macht man so weiter damit.
Wenn eine Kartoffel was zur anderen sagt, dann sagt sie:
      Ich möchte nicht gegessen werden.
Wenn sie noch was sagen kann, dann kann sie sagen:
      In der Erde war es besser.
Wenn man das jetzt so weiter macht, dann macht man so weiter.

THE POEM TRAVELS THROUGH A BODY
AND DOESN'T EVEN NOD HELLO

I

When one travels through a country, it is a country worth travelling through.
When one leaves a settled home town, one settles for another home town.
When one finishes writing a poem, one writes another poem.
If that is a joy, then that is a joy.
If one is drinking a beer, then one is drinking a beer.
If that is a pleasure, then it is a pleasure.
When I start talking like this, I keep talking like this.
When I eat franks & beans, then I eat franks & and I eat beans.
If one calls that joy, then it is joy.
When one uses one's life for material, then one's life becomes material.
When one wishes to invent a grammar, one feels free.
When one wishes to implant a new perception, one plants.
If one wishes to pound, one wishes to pound.
When one continues like this, then one is continuing like this.
When a potato speaks to another potato, it says, *I don't want to be eaten.*
When it says something else, it says, *it was better in the dirt.*
If one keeps going on like this, then one keeps going.

2

Fährt man von der Quelle zu den Leuchttürmen, fährt man nicht
     von den Leuchttürmen zur Quelle.
Rede ich über Brackwasser, rede ich nicht über Hochseefischerei.
Rede ich über Algebra, was ich nie mache, rede ich über etwas,
     von dem ich nichts verstehe.
Rede ich über das Wetter, kann ich darüber reden.
Rede ich über Fotografie, habe ich eine Ahnung davon.
Rede ich über Theater, weiß ich zu wenig, um darüber reden zu können.
Rede ich über Gedichte, denke ich, ich sollte nicht darüber reden.
Schreibe ich Gedichte, schreibe ich Gedichte.
Schreibt man Gedichte, genügt das.
Fährt man von der Quelle zu den Leuchttürmen, dann macht man das.
Wird man pathetisch, dann muss die Heide brennen.
Wird man leise, wird man leise.
Stellt man sich eine Schreibaufgabe, hat man eine Schreibkrise.
Hat man eine Schreibkrise, sollte man seine Zeit mit anderem verbringen.
Sagt man Krise, sollte ein Land brennen.
Schreibt man ein Gedicht, dann schreibt man es.
Schreibt man keins, dann schreibt man keins.
Sagt man immer wieder man, weiß irgendwann niemand mehr,
     wer gemeint ist.
Sagt man immer wieder man, meint man nur sich selbst.
Sagt man immer wieder man, sind alle gemeint.
Sage ich immer wieder wir, sagt irgendwann jemand, ich bin nicht dein
     wir, mein Großvater wollte niemals auf eine DGB-Demo schießen.
Fährt man von der Quelle zu den Leuchttürmen, schwimmen Lachse mit.
Fährt man von den Leuchttürmen zur Quelle, schwimmen Lachse mit.

II

If one strolls from fountains to lighthouses, one is not strolling from
        lighthouses to fountains.
If I speak of brackish water, I am not speaking about all the fish in the sea.
If I speak of algebra, which I won't, I am speaking of ideas I don't
        understand.
When I talk about the weather, well, I talk just fine about that.
If I talk about photography, I'm talking with a clue.
If I talk about theatre, I don't know what I'm talking about.
If I talk about poems, I shouldn't be talking.
When I write poems, I write poems.
If one writes poems, that is good enough.
If one wanders from fountains to lighthouses, from fountains to
        lighthouses one wanders.
If one wallows in melodrama then the heath & heather must burn.
When one goes quiet, one goes quiet.
If one gives oneself a 'writing exercise', one has a 'writing emergency'.
When one says 'emergency', a country sparks.
If one has a 'writing emergency', one ought to visit with friends.
If one writes a poem, then one writes a poem.
If one writes no poems, then one writes no poems.
If no one writes a poem, then no one writes a poem.
If one keeps saying 'one' then eventually no one knows which 'one' is
        meant.
If one keeps saying 'one', one means only oneself.
If one keeps saying 'one', everyone is meant.
Whenever I say 'we' someone raises an eyebrow and says, 'We are not we –
        my grandfather wasn't spurring horses into picket lines.'
If one travels from fountains to lighthouses, salmon still swim.
If one travels from lighthouses to fountains, salmon still swim.

3

Ich weiß, dass Kunst nur die traurige Zusammenballung aller Defizite ist.
Ich weiß, dass mir dieser Gedanke sehr logisch erscheint.
Ich weiß, dass ich mit diesem Gedanken Gedichte schreibe.
Ich weiß, dass ich Menschen, die Gedichte schreiben und sich öffentlich
    über Gedichte im Allgemeinen äußern, merkwürdig finde.
Ich weiß, dass ich haupt- oder nebenberufliche Kritiker von Gedichten
    merkwürdig finde, weil sie eine Vorstellung von dem haben, was
    ein Gedicht sein soll.
Ich habe mal in einem französischen Film eine Strandszene gesehen, in
    der ein Mann einer Frau sagte: »Madame, ich möchte mit ihrer
    Tochter schlafen. Es soll wie ein Gedicht sein, was ich ihnen
    widme.«
Ich weiß nicht, was ein Gedicht ist.
Ich weiß, dass jemand, der sich für einen großen oder wichtigen Dichter
    hält, einen Knall hat.
Ich weiß, dass jedes größere Kind ein Gedicht schreiben kann.
Ich weiß, dass Jugendliche Gedichte schreiben.
Ich weiß, dass ich erwachsen bin und immer noch Gedichte schreibe.
Ich weiß, dass jedes Gedicht die Ballung aller Defizite ist.
Ich habe mal geschrieben, dass ich das mit »Bier« betitelte Gedicht von
    Karl Mickel über die Alpen tragen würde, um den Fortbestand
    dieses Gedichts zu sichern.
Ich weiß, dass ich die Alpen falsch einschätze.
Ich weiß, dass jedes Gedicht traurig ist.
Ich weiß, dass ich keine Traurigkeit über die Alpen tragen möchte.
Ich weiß, dass ich Gedichte schreibe, weil ich Gedichte schreiben will.
Ich weiß, dass diese Logik bahnbrechend ist.

III

I understand that art is only the sad tallying of deficits.
I know this thought seems obvious and logical to me.
I know I write my poems with this in mind.
I know people who speak openly about their poems are strangers to me.
I know I find critics strange because they have ideas about what a poem
      should be.
Once, I saw a French film where a man on a beach proposes to a woman
      on a beach: 'Madame,' he said, 'I would like to sleep with your
      daughter. It will be a poem I dedicate to you.'
I do not know what a poem is.
I know anyone who considers themselves to be an important poet has a
      hole in their head.
I know any kid can write poems.
I know teenagers write poems.
I know that I am an adult, still, I write poems.
I know every poem is an accounting of deficits.
I know I once wrote that I would carry the poem 'Snow' by Sarah Broom
      over the Alps to ensure its eternal existence in the hearts and
      minds of readers everywhere.
I know that every poem is sad.
I know I do not want to carry any more sadness over the Alps.
I understand I have lied to myself about how big the Alps are.
I know I write poems because I want to write poems.
I know, with this logic, I too am a mountaineer.

4

Das Gedicht grenzt im Westen an die Vereinigten Staaten der Zwecklosigkeit.
Das Gedicht grenzt im Osten an eine freiwillige Feuerwehr.
Das Gedicht grenzt im Süden an eine Tüte Bio-Mehl.
Das Gedicht grenzt im Norden an subventionierte Kinderbetreuung.
Das Gedicht grenzt, wenn es Grenzen hat, an seine Selbstgefälligkeit.
Das Gedicht geht durch einen Körper.
Das Gedicht geht durch meinen Körper.
Das Gedicht geht durch meinen Körper und grüßt nicht mal.
Das Gedicht holt sich, was es braucht.
Das Gedicht braucht Jahre, zwei Minuten.
Das Gedicht wird manchmal richtig scheiße.
Das Gedicht wird dann gelöscht.
Das Gedicht ist so dämlich wie der, der darüber redet, darüber schreibt.
Das Gedicht ist so klug wie der, der ins Museum geht.
Das Gedicht braucht keine Schlaumeierei, keine Milchmädchenrechnung.
Das Gedicht braucht kein Schreiben über das Gedicht.
Das Gedicht will geschrieben, will gemacht werden.
Das Gedicht will nicht geschrieben, will nicht gemacht werden.
Das Gedicht ist ein Hüttenkäse.
Das Gedicht will sagen: Lasst mich in Ruhe, wenn ich fertig bin.
Das Gedicht will sagen: In der Ziege war es besser.
Das Gedicht will sagen: Woher weißt du, was ich will und warum kann ich
        überhaupt reden.

IV

The poem requires a visa to enter the United States of Aimlessness.
The poem requires a visa to enter the volunteer fire department.
The poem is stopped on the border of a sack of stoneground organic flour.
The poem is stopped on the border of subsidized child care.
The poem enforces it's own borders drawn straight from its own smugness.
The poem travels like a diplomat through a body.
The poem travels through my body.
The poem travels through my body and doesn't even nod hello.
The poem takes what it needs.
The poem needs years, a couple of minutes.
The poem is a piece of shit sometimes.
The poem is then deleted.
The poem is as dim-witted as the one who writes about it, talks about it.
The poem is as clever as one who reads labels at museums.
The poem doesn't need one's smart-alec, nor one's Pollyanna.
The poem turns a deaf ear to your praise, your critique.
The poem wants to be written, to be made.
The poem does not want to be written, to be made.
The poem is cottage cheese.
The poem wants to say, *it was warmer inside the cow.*
The poem wants to say, *leave me alone, I'll be written when I'm in my right mind.*
The poem wants to say, *how would you know what I want and why would I ever
      speak to you?*

5

Ich schreibe, wenn etwas kommt.

Ich schreibe, wenn etwas nicht kommt.

Ich schreibe, wenn etwas ankommt

Ich schreibe, wenn etwas nicht ankommt.

Ich schreibe, wenn die Defizite.

Ich schreibe, wenn auf einem T-Shirt steht »I'm a muslim, not a bomb«.

Ich schreibe, wenn die Tiefe, die Höhe, das Dazwischen.

Ich schreibe, wenn die Apnoe-Taucher, die Speedclimber.

Ich schreibe, wenn diese verdammten Schmerztiere.

Ich schreibe, wenn diese Verwahrlosung.

Ich schreibe, wenn dieses Dieses.

Ich schreibe, wenn die Schönheit eines Feldes.

Ich schreibe, wenn das Schweigen, die Stille.

Ich schreibe, wenn die Defizite.

Ich schreibe, wenn das gefrostete Stück Wiese vor einem Familienhaus.

Ich schreibe, wenn die Heide brennt.

Ich schreibe, wenn das Land brennt.

Ich schreibe, wenn die Hochstuhlrocker, die Badewannenwasser-Kapitäne.

Ich schreibe, wenn die Liebe, der Hass, die Leere undsoweiter.

Ich schreibe, wenn der von Schnee bedeckte, an der Ampel wartende Hund
und seine Ahnungslosigkeit.

Ich schreibe, wenn größere Aufmerksamkeit versprochen wird.

Ich schreibe, wenn Geld geboten wird.

V

I write when something comes
I write when something does not come
I write when something comes back
I write when something does not come back
I write when the t-shirt says 'I'm a muslim, not a bomb'
I write when the deficits
I write when the depths, the heights, the inbetweens
I write when the crushed lungs of free-divers, the flaming legs of fell runners
I write when these terminal pain junkies
I write when this self-neglect
I write when This
I write when the waving beauty of a field
I write when the shhhh, the silence
I write when the deficits
I write when the frosted front garden
I write when the heath burns
I write when the country burns
I write when children rock out in their high chairs
I write when rubber ducky brings the fun
I write when the love, the hate, the emptiness, the etcetera, etcetera, etcetera
I write when the snow-dusted dog stands clueless as the green man returns
        to red
I write when the circulation is healthy, the broadcast wide
I write when money is on the table

6

Ich antworte, ich schreibe sie mit den Händen.

Ich antworte, ich lebe zeitweise und teilweise davon und damit und gut und danke.

Ich antworte, dass ich darauf nicht antworten werde, Sie fragen doch auch keinen Roman-Autor, warum er keine Gedichte schreibt.

Ich antworte, dass jedes Hoch- oder Flachhaus mehr Erotik hat.

Ich antworte, dass jedes geschlossene Gewässer mehr von allem hat.

Ich antworte, dass ein Feuerwehrfest in Posemuckel mehr Menschen erfreut.

Ich antworte, dass diese Tätigkeit mehr Lächerlichkeit hat als ein Feuerwehrfest in Posemuckel.

Ich antworte, dass diese Tätigkeit mehr Ernsthaftigkeit hat als ein Feuerwehrfest in Posemuckel.

Ich antworte, dass ich etwas mache, was Jugendliche tun.

Ich antworte, dass das eine Fehlschaltung ist.

Ich antworte, dass es ein Handwerk ist.

Ich antworte, ich bin manchmal glücklich dabei.

Ich antworte, ich schreibe sie mit den Händen.

VI

I answer: I write by hand.

I answer: sometimes and partly and I don't order steak every night but I
eat OK thank you very much.

I answer: any squat building, any skyscraper is more erotic than
metaphor.

I answer: a still pond holds more of anything, more everything.

I answer: because of a faulty circuit.

I answer: a firefighter's festival in Dingwall offers more joy to the world.

I answer: a firefighter's festival in Dingwall doesn't take itself so seriously.

I answer: a firefighter's festival in Dingwall is less ludicrous than this act.

I answer with a question: why doesn't the novelist write a poem?

I answer: I do what teenagers do.

I answer: sometimes it does make me happy.

I answer: this is craft.

I answer: I make them by hand.

RYAN VAN WINKLE

It is a strange and scary thing to be responsible for someone's voice, for their representation in another language. Bjorn's voice was a pleasure to have in my head, so much so that it reappears regularly.

BJÖRN KUHLIGK

Lieber Ryan,
ich mochte es, mit Deinen Gedichten zu fechten und nicht immer gewinnen zu können. Ich mochte es, Deine Gedichte ins Deutsche herüberzuholen. Ich mochte es, dass wir eine Arbeit taten, von der wir so wenig verstanden, und dass wir uns jede Menge Mühe gaben. Ich mochte Deine Krawatte, die du selbst bei gefühlten 45 Grad Celsius trugst, Deinen Koffer, der schon die halbe Welt gesehen haben muss, und nun endlich auch den Elektronik-Markt am Alexanderplatz.
Auf bald bei einem Gemüse-Smoothie,
Björn

RYAN VAN WINKLE

Es ist schon eine seltsame und auch beängstigende Angelegenheit, für die Stimme eines anderen verantwortlich zu sein und für deren Darstellung in einer anderen Sprache. Björns Stimme hatte ich jedoch gerne in meinem Kopf zu Gast – so sehr, dass sie regelmäßig wieder auftaucht.

BJÖRN KUHLIGK

Dear Ryan,
I liked fencing with your poems without always being able to win. I liked hauling your poems over into German. I liked it that we did a job about which we understood so little, and that we made such a huge effort. I liked your tie, which you even wore in what felt like 45 degree Celsius weather; your suitcase, which must have already seen half the world, and now, finally, the electronics store at Alexanderplatz as well.

See you soon over a vegetable smoothie,
Björn

PETER MACKAY }

interpreter }
Sprachmittler }

{ DAGMARA KRAUS

{ Joseph Given

NEW WORLD

With her memory failing she would pour
the first whisky of the evening three times
and see skulls piled up in the armchairs,
mottled with age like the cat dead ten years,
and turn with the fear of her life to her husband
who would again be not there not there.

They never got round to heating the upstairs,
and now duvets and masking tape close off the stairwell
with the bedframes of flitting tenants,
and the Paisley carpets fester in the damp
in the room where, one childhood summer,
she played me Dvořák over and over again,
his *New World Symphony* filling
the one room in the house that faced the sea.

Which would forever be the open sea.

NEW WORLD

A cuimhne a' fàilligeadh, dhòirteadh i
a' chiad dram dhen oidhche trup 's trup
agus chitheadh i càrn de chlaigeannan
air an t-sòfa, riabhan 's breac mar a' chat
a bhàsaich o chionn deich bliadhna,
agus thionndadh i ann an eagal a beatha
dha a fear-pòsta nach robh, a-rithist, an sin an sin.

Cha robh teas ann riamh shuas an staidhre
agus tha an talla a-nis dùinte le duvetan
's frèamaichean-leapa luchd-màil sgaogach,
agus tha bratan Phàislig a' grodadh san fhliche
anns an t-seòmar far an do chluich i,
aon samhradh m' òige, Dvořák dhomh trup
's a rithist, an *New World Symphony* a' lìonadh
an aon t-seòmair san taigh le sealladh na mara.

Agus le sin bha i a' ciallachadh na mara làn.

AUS DER NEUEN WELT

Als das Gedächtnis sie im Stich zu lassen drohte,
goss sie drei Mal ihren ersten Whisky ein
und sah Schädel sich auf Sesseln türmen,
altersfleckig wie der tote Kater,
und wandte sich in Todesangst an ihren Mann,
der schon wieder fort und weg war.

Sie kamen nie dazu, den oberen Stock noch
zu beheizen und stopften den Treppenschacht
mit Decken aus und Malerkrepp und mit Gestellen
von Mieterbetten; es verfaulte in der Moderluft
der Perserläufer in dem Raum, wo sie Dvořak
eines Kindheitssommers rauf und runterspielte:
Aus der neuen Welt erfüllte das einzige im Haus
dem offenen Meer ganz zugewandte Zimmer.

Für immer war da offenes Meer.

IN CORDOBA

While I am waiting with my camera ready
for you to let your robe fall to the floor,

I will think of plantations of pine dark
and surrounded by a trodden-down fence

a laugh from the second floor, a glimpse of skin
dun-fair through the shutters

white linen hanging from white balconies
through thousands of dust motes

gap-toothed smiles in the shadows of cloisters,
the smell of milk-thistle rotting in patios

and I would touch you, my love, at arm's length,
leave prints in our sweat on the walls.

ANN AN CORDOBA

Fhad 's a bhios mi a' feitheamh, deiseil, lem chamara
gus an leig thu le do ròb tuiteam dhan làr

bidh mi a' smaoineachadh air planntachas giuthais duirch
air a chuartachadh le feansa shaltraichte

gàire on dàrna ùrlar 's plathadh de chraicinn
bhàn-donn air cùl nan siutairean

lìon-anart geal a' crochadh o fhor-uinneagan
ann am mìltean de dhùradain

mìog chabach ann an dubhair nan clabhstairean
fàileadh iadh-luis a' grodadh sa *phatio*,

's bheanainn riut, a ghràidh, le barr mo mheòirean:
dh'fhàgainn làraich corraigean nar n-allas air a' bhalla.

IN CÓRDOBA

Während ich so mit offener Blende warte,
dass du dein Kleid zu Boden fallen lässt,

will ich an Schonungen denken, Pinien, dunkle,
und umzingelt vom zertretenen Zaun,

an das Lachen aus dem zweiten Stock, ans Haut
Erhaschen, der sepiagelben durchs Spalett,

bleiche Laken, die vom bleichen Austritt hängen
in tausend Stäuben, an das Lächeln

in den Klosterschatten und die Lücke in den Zähnen,
wie die Fieberdistel riecht, faulend in den Höfen

und dass ich Dich berührte, Liebes, dass wir
im Schweiß an Mauern unsere Spuren ließen.

PETER MACKAY

IN THE BRITISH MUSEUM

We pass from room to room
taking selfies
in mimic poses
occasionally catching the originals
reflected in the glass:

Venus surprised at her bath,
Dionysus and his panther,
Dionysus and his ithyphallic satyrs,
the ram in the thicket from Ur,
Takhebhkeman, the beserker with his teeth,

and on those marbles,
buttressed, bruised, ordered, in state,
the hundred horses rearing in terror
bearing their decapitated riders
through walls that are pervious, impervious.

ANN AN ARD-MHUSEAUM BHREATAINN

Gabh sinn oirnn, o sheòmar gu seòmar,
a' togail selfie-an
ann an cumaidhean fhanaideach
a' faighinn corra plathaidhean
dhen bun-dealbhan sna lòsan:

Venus a' blaomadh san amar
Dionysus agus a phanthair
agus a bhoc-dheamhan ithyphallic
an rùda sa phreas à Ur
Takhebkheman 's am fear-tàileisg na bhoile

agus air a' mharmor ud, an dèidh lidrigeadh
agus droinneadh, nan taigh-aire,
a' cheud each, a' bocadh le uamhas,
a' giùlain marcaichean gun chinn
tro bhallachan pòrach, neo-phòrach.

IM BRITISH MUSEUM

Wir laufen von einem Saal zum anderen,
machen Selfies
in Nachäffposen
und erwischen hier und da die Spiegelung
eines Originals im Glas:

die Venus, im Bade überrascht,
Dionysos und seinen Panther,
Dionysos und seine ithyphallischen Satyrn, den
Schafbock im Dickicht aus Ur, Takhebkhenem,
den Berserker mit seinen Zähnen,

und, in Marmor,
gestützt, geprellt, geordnet, aufgebahrt,
die vor Schreck aufgebäumten hundert Pferde,
die geköpfte Reiter tragen
quer durch Wände, durchlässige, undurchlässig.

PETER MACKAY

WHEN I THINK OF THE INCOMMUNICABLE

I think of *The Coffee Pot*
with its white formica tables,
the glut & clot of beans & sausage & chips,
the adult voices, alien in their languages,
in a broth of *achs* and *Thioraidhs* and *maebes*,
and the way you'd fill a glass with Coke
to the brim and the fizz would dance
like sugarplum fairies above the black

or of a crop sprayer near Anstruther,
a green and yellow sunburst *Air Ride*,
carting diamonds, good-for-nothing rainbows,
from pillar to post, or back again,
depending how you look at it

NUAIR A SMAOINEACHAS MI AIR NA THA DO-THUIGSINNEACH

bidh mi a' smaoineachadh air *The Coffee Pot*,
leis a bhùird gheail formica,
glut 's geir pònaireain, isbeanain 's *chips*,
guthan inbhich, cèin nan cainnt,
brot *ach* 's *Thioraidh* 's *maebe*,
an dòigh a lionadh tu glainne Choke dham bile
agus dhannsadh nan curracagan
mar shìthichean siùcair os cionn an duibh,

air neo tractor faisg air Anstruther,
a' spreidheadh achaidhean,
Air Ride sunburst buidhe-uaine,
a' gualain daoimeanan, boghachan-froise gun fheum,
eadar a' chlach san sgrath neo air ais a-rithist
a rèir 's mar a choimheadas tu air

WENN ICH AN DAS UNVERMITTELBARE DENKE

denke ich an *The Coffee Pot*,
an Tische aus weißem Resopal,
das Getriefe & Geklumpe von Bohnen & Wurst & Fritten,
Stimmen von Erwachsenen, die fremd in ihren Sprachen sind,
in dem Brei aus *Achs*, *Thioraidhs* und *Maebes*,
und ich denke an die Art, auf die du ein Glas Cola
randvoll machst und das Sprudeln dann
wie Zuckerfeen überm Schwarz auftanzt,

oder ich stelle mir die Selbstfahrspritze bei Anstruther vor,
die grüngelbe, Funkeln sprühende, Marke *Air Ride*,
diese Karre der Brillanten, nutzloser Regenbögen,
wie sie von A nach B fährt, oder umgekehrt,
je nachdem, wie man es sieht

THE LEAK

The cistern is leaking –
through the boards the water flows,
a tacky rusted water
percolated through dust & wood & iron.

This, or something like this,
is what flows in you, in your renal system,
in your veins:
water that has put on time & weight.

It drips, a boozy oracle,
reveals unofficial secrets
of what lives between motes, in cracks,
that forthelifeofyou should not be seen.

AN T-AOIDEAN

Tha an sisteal a' snigheadh –
tro na bùird tha an t-uisge na ruith,
uisge ronnach ruadh
air drùidheadh tro stùr 's iarann 's fiodh.

Tha seo, neo rudeigin coltach ris,
a' ruith tromhad, nad dubhain,
nad chuislean:
uisge le uallach tìd 's cuideim.

Tha e a' sileadh, oracail le smùid air,
a' taisbeanadh rùintean-dìomhair an-oifigeil
na tha beò eadar dùrdain, ann an sgàinidhean,
nach bu chòir fhacinn ridobheò.

DAS LECK

Die Zisterne leckt –
es fließt Wasser durch die Bretter,
ein zähes Wasser voller Rost,
geseiht durch Staub & Holz & Eisen.

Das, oder etwas in dieser Art
ist, was in dir fließt, in deinen Nieren,
in deinen Venen:
ein Wasser, das an Gewicht & Zeit gewann.

Dies versoffene Orakel tropft,
gibt Vertrauliches dessen preis,
was inmitten Stäuben & in Rissen wohnt;
es soll umallesinderwelt bloß nicht zutage treten.

DAGMARA KRAUS }

interpreter }
Sprachmittler }

{ **PETER MACKAY**

{ Joseph Given

DAGMARA KRAUS

NUR MUT, MOND

(für ein kind)

> Ich verstehe nicht, wie man Gedichte
> über den Mond schreiben kann ...
> *Zbigniew Herbert*

fast fipsig: der mondspion, das zwergen
mal der mitternacht; ein perlensprenkel,
sonnezwistig, listig, lausig angefacht

weltab; ein klicker, eisstein, flohnst du
glarend übers große rad – fadenöse, lose,
waise, am gestärkten kragen kahler nacht

flugsand? blesse? hat nicht david dich da
hochgeschafft, mit der schleuder, himmels
tresse, orion um den ruhm gebracht ?

hab den nachtflor ausgemessen, mir einen
fummel draus gemacht; mit der brosche,
deinem halo, allen stoff des alls gerafft –

ach wie die gammaeulen neiden ... und
der verkrachte goliath, dem du trendelstern
die stirne kreidelst, hat jetzt doppelt keine macht

BE BRAVE, MOON

(for a child)

> I don't know how people can
> write poems about the moon
> *Zbigniew Herbert*

so teensy: this spying-moon, dwarfish
midnight mole; a pearlsplatter,
sun-feuding, shrewd and crudely lit

a world away; a marble of ice-gneiss, you stravaiged
glaring over the whole sky-wheel – a sloppy orphaned
popper on the starched collar of bald night

sand-drift? little horse blaze? didn't David
fling you up there with his sling – O heaven's
braid – and steal Orion's fame?

i've measured out the night-lace, made myself
a stole from it; with your halo
brooch, i bunched up the stuff of the whole universe –

och, how envious are the moths ... and
that wannabe Goliath, on whose heid you chalkillied
a saunterstar, has twice nothing your power

3 FATRASIEN

#1

nehmen wir einmal an
das vogelmot schlich
mit geknickter schnute
vielleicht sogar leicht eingestochen
und das doch mit guter vorsichtigkeit
halb von auswärts
und in lange schweife verschlungen
zum domestizierten mund
handelten säfte verborgen und eilends
von der zeitstellung
dieser widrigkeiten

DAGMARA KRAUS | PETER MACKAY

3 FANTRASIES

1

so let us consider now
the birdword that sneaks
its crooked and maybe dented beak
with all due caution
from outwards halfway in
and tangled in its own antitail
towards the domesticated mouth
then consuming themselves
hidden and hasting
the humours would convey
the chronosite of these obstacles

beachdaicheamaid ma-ta
gun do snàig an eunfhacail
le a bheilleag eagach
tolgte 's dòcha gu h-aotrom
agus fiù 's gu h-iongantach fhaiceallach
leth-slighe a-staigh on a-mach
ann an earballlùib fhada shnàgte
a dh'ionnsaigh a' bheòil challaichte
's le sin dheanadh an leanntras deannta 's air a chleith
malairt le làraicheantìd'
nan cnapan-starra-sa

so let us consider
that the wordfowl crept
with its petted lip notched
maybe gently scratched
and even nailfully cautious
halfway in from outwards
tangled in a long tailcurve
towards the domesticated mouth
and with that the humours hurrying and hidden
would barter the timetracks
of these stumbling blocks

2

durch die tode des testanten zogen
als fußwärmer pfeifvögel fronten
er war schillernd in allen veralienirt
maximale wasser waren passiert
gerissen konnten die älteren
den hohen fuß der ursache
am horizont mit harz versehen
wenn die glashäfen langsam schwanken
ehe abschluss seine hände wusch
ist er deutlich
an der tischdecke abzuwischen

2

through the testamenter's deaths flew
a front of foot-warm whistling-birds
in them he was iridescentransmogrified
passing beyond the ends of the waters
the older cunning ones
could apply resin to the high stand
of the cause on the horizon
when the glass harbours sway softly
before completion washed its hands
it is obviously
to be wiped off on the tablecloth

tro bhàis a' thiomnaiche theich
eòin fheadanach chas-teasach aig aghaidh
unnta uile bha e sionn 's air chaochladh
seachad air fìor-iomall nan uisgeachan
b'urrainn dha na feadhainn seòlta na sine
bìth a lìbhrigeadh air fàire
air cois àrd na cuise
nuair luaisg na callachan glainne gu socair
mus do nì iomlanachd a làmhan
tha aige ri bhith
suathadh gu follaiseach air anart a' bhùird

through the testamenter's deaths flew
itchyfeet whistling birds in a v
in them he was changelinged and lustrous
beyond the very ends of the waters
the older craftier ones
could administer birdlime on the horizon
to the high stem of the cause
when the glass harbours rock softly
before completeness washes its hands
it must obviously
be wiped off on the table linen

3

ein turm kniff ziemlich pelikan
aus drei kugeln deutlich feucht
sie fanden die den grund verband
war verbren weißes porzellan
am hafenton zerbrochen
und restwas das mit glut versorgt
noch kett nicht ihre tülle an
weils zauberwort vom ammenhang
fast fünfzehn einfache flinten
und gut zwei paar kutschen
zu stark dafür ist kleine blase

3

a pelican clipped heavily by a tower
visibly damp from three orbs
they found combined in her the ground
a verb-deer of white porcelain
shattered in the harbour's notes
and the trace feeds it with embers
do not tie down her tulle
because the magic word ontext
is almost fifteen simple shotguns
and two good pairs of carriages
too strong for that, little bulge

peileagan air giorradh gu mòr le tùr
gu follaiseach tais o thrì chruinnichean
lorg iad co-cheangailte innt' an grunnd
gnìomhairfèidh obair-chrèadha ghil
na spealgan ann an suaim a' chala
's tha am mar-thà-fiamh na ghrìosadh
na cuibhrich a tulle
leis gu bheil an t-seun co-theac
cha mhòr coig gunna-froise deug
agus dà phaidhear charbad
ro laidir son sin, a bhuilg bhig

a pelican curtailed by a tower
clearly damp from three globes
they found bound in her the ground
a verbdeer of white ceramics
in fragments in the sound of the port
and the alreadytrace is stirring the ashes
don't fetter her tulle
since lism the magic spell
is almost fifteen shotguns
and two pairs of broughams
too strong for that, o little blister

TRISKELE

der grüne baumpython ist ausgezogen
es webt sich keine schlinge ums gelege
das raue hauthemd hat er mitgenommen
er hatte sonst nichts zu vererben
und hängt jetzt turban hoch im edenbaum

der grüne baumpython ist ausgezogen
er hinterließ nur ein paar klumpen erde
auf welchem friedhof ist er beigesetzt
hat die hyäne ihn gefressen
die heut so faul im schatten pennt

der grüne baumpython ist ausgezogen
leer bleibt die gitterklause ohne licht
wie froh sind alle klauen krallen pfoten
allein sein raum im zoo trägt trauer
hat pythons jade angenommen

ein grüner raumpython ist eingezogen
ich floh apophis und res kähne
direkt in rereks schlangenbauch
verfolg dort faucher durchs gehege
sie führen mich in adams traum:

der müde baumpython war ausgezogen

TRISKELION

the green tree-python's moved out
it weaves no noose round its clutch
it has taken with it the rough skinshirt
which is all it has to pass down
and turban-hangs high in a heaventree

the green tree-python's moved out
has left just a few clods of dirt
is he buried in some grave
was he eaten up by the hyena
that naps lazy today in the shade

the green tree-python's moved out
its lattice cell's empty and dark
how happy the claws talons nails
in the zoo just one house mourns
decked in the snake's cast-off jade

a green room-python's moved in
i fled from Apep and Re's boats
straight into Rekrek's snakegut
and chasing snarlthings in their hutch
i fall into Adam's dream:

the tired tree-python's moved out

TRISKELION

tha a' chraobh-paithean òiruain' air imrich
chan fhìgh i crampag mun chuairt a h-àl
thug i leatha a lèine-bèin gharbh
an aon dìleab a chrochas i às dèidh
turban-àrd ann an nèamh-craoibh'

tha a' chraobh-paithean òiruain' air imrich
air corra clod ùir fhàgail air a cùl
ciod an cladh sa bheil i tìodhlaichte
an deach i glàmadh leis a' haidheana
a' gabhail norrag a-nis leisg sa sgàil

tha a' chraobh-paithean òiruain' air imrich
a cill chliathach falamh 's dorch'
cho toilichte ann an cròg spòg 's spàgan
chan eil ach aon taigh na chaoidh sa sù
sgeadaichte ann an òirghlas na paithein

tha saobh-paithean òiruain' air inimrich
theich mi o dh'Apep 's luing Re
calg-dhìreach gu brù-nathrach Rekrek
tron t-saobhaidh 's mi air tòir dreamrud
bheireadh iad mi gu aisling Àdhaimh:

tha a' chraobh-paithean sgìth air imrich

TRISKELION

the greengold tree-python's moved out
she won't weave a noose round her eggs
she's taken away her pelt-shirt
the one gift she'll have to pass on
and turban-hangs high in a heaventree

the greengold tree-python's moved out
leaving behind her loam-clods
in what ditch is it she's buried
was she eaten up by the hyena
that naps lazy now in the shade

the greengold tree-python's moved out
its barred cell's empty and dark
so happy the claws paws and talons
only one house laments in the zoo
decked in the python's goldgrey

a greengold wrong-python's moved in
i fled from Apep and Re's boats
spearstraight into Rekrek's snakestomach
chasing snarlthings in their den
i fall into the dreams of Adam:

the tired tree-python's moved out

PETER MACKAY

The reVERSible workshops were a fantastic experience: intense, precise and occasionally raucous carryings-through and across from German into English and Gaelic. It was a great pleasure to translate, but also to work with Dagmara. Her use of language was so playfully exacting, with each word an elusive chimera, hovering between different words or ideas in the German; the challenge was to try and find not a translation, but a fitting parallel foray into my own languages, to see where they would take us. I hope my own poems came close finding places as strange and new as the worlds Dagmara's poems create.

DAGMARA KRAUS

Schottisches Gälisch? Nie gehört. *Hab ne Couch in'n Ohren.* Verstanden davon nur Laute, die sich hier und da zu Verständlichem formten. *Hier, Homer, du Schwanzchô-meur – für dich. Aber Sinn? Da tockelts Elfchen.* Jedenfalls schrieb ich mit und auf, was von Peters gälischer Lesung während der Werkstatt zu mir durchdrang: *Onan, komm, wir gehn, Annas 'czochy [holen]; is' eh fein, so'n Codegott mit Äpplein und Neurosen.* Joseph, mein Mitübersetzer, nahm Peters Lesung auf, so dass ich sie später noch einmal hören könnte: *Finesse, nech, schwimmt in Rüstung, färbt Nicies.* Schließlich hatte ich neben »echten« Übersetzungen der englischen Gedichte auch eine homophone eines gälischen ausprobieren wollen (denn ohne Interlinearvorgaben seitens eines Übersetzers war den gälischen Texten nicht anders als homophon beizukommen). *Esse – selbst Panda – Panther, fand er; ess auch den Fockgewinn, ess den fallig und rud.* Zuhause hörte ich die Aufnahmen nochmals durch und notierte, nicht ohne Verwunderung über die vielen Protagonisten, die sich in Peters Gedichten plötzlich zu tummeln begannen. *Da rottet sie, die Fresshaaruhr.* Verstünde Peter mein vergälischtes Deutsch, wenn ich ihm diese Notizen zu einem seiner Gedichte einmal vorläse? *Hemmens mich, übersetz ichs in Jolle, das ist 'ne Wärmerette.* Hörte er sich sprechen? *Kriechkriech zum Thron hin, bock-ekliger Urwisch, [ich] tratrat mal durchs Walken, die ganze Harferei.* Aber warum denn so obszön? *Dann riecht ihm der Po noch durchs Wollloch.*

PETER MACKAY

Die VERSschmuggel-Workshops waren eine wunderbare Erfahrung: intensives, prä-
zises und zuweilen lautes Übertragen vom Deutschen ins Englische und Gälische. Mit
Dagmara zu arbeiten und sie zu übersetzen war ein großes Vergnügen. Ihr Sprachum-
gang ist so spielerisch genau, jedes Wort gleicht einer beziehungsreichen Chimäre, die
zwischen verschiedenen Wörtern oder Ideen im Deutschen schwebt; die Herausforde-
rung bestand darin, nicht eine Übersetzung zu finden, sondern eine passende Parallele
in meinen eigenen Sprachen, und zu sehen, wohin uns das führen würde. Ich hoffe,
dass meine eigenen Gedichte es geschafft haben, genauso fremdartige und neue Orte
zu finden wie die Welten, die Dagmaras Gedichte erschaffen.

DAGMARA KRAUS

Scottish Gaelic? Never heard of it. *Got a couch in m'ears.* I only understood sounds,
which here and there took on comprehensible forms. *Here, Homer, you cockchômeur
– for you.* But sense? *It's trulling elfies.* In any case, I wrote down the things that made
their way through to me from Peter's Gaelic reading during the workshop: *Onan, come,
we're going to [pick up] Anna's hoseys; 'tis fine anyway, such a codegod with lil' apple and
neuroses.* Joseph, my co-translator, recorded Peter's reading so that I could listen to it
again later: *Finesse, nowt, swims in armour, colours nicies.* In the end, alongside the "real"
translations of the English poems, I also wanted to try out a homophonic translation of
a Gaelic one (since without the interlinear guide from a translator, the only way I could
get at the Gaelic was homophonically). *Eat – I, myself a panda – a panther, said he; and eat
them breath-earning, eat them fallish and rude.* At home I listened to the recordings once
more and noted down – not without amazement – the many protagonists who suddenly began to bustle about in Peter's poems. *There she rots, the clock-scoffing-hair.* Were
I to read him these notes on one of his poems, would Peter understand my faux-gaeli-
cized German? *Are y'obstructing me, I translate it into dinghy, that's a warmth-redeemer.*
Would he hear himself speaking? *Crawl-crawling toward the throne, goat-gross, primal
hogwash, [I] kickicked through the filling, the whole harpery.* But then, why so obscene? *His
bottom still smelling through the wool-hole.*

ANNA CROWE }

interpreter }
Sprachmittlerin }

{ **ODILE KENNEL**

{ Katy Derbyshire

ANNA CROWE

A CALENDER OF HARES
for Valerie Gillies

1. At the raw end of winter
the mountain is half snow, half
dun grass. Only when snow
moves does it become a hare.

2. If you can catch a hare
and look into its eye,
you will see the whole world.

3. That day in March
watching two hares boxing
at the field's edge, she felt
the child quicken.

4. It is certain Midas never saw a hare
or he would not have lusted after gold.

5. When the buzzard wheels
like a slow kite overhead
the hare pays out the string.

6. The man who tells you
he has thought of everything
has forgotten the hare.

7. The hare's form, warm yet empty.
Stumbling upon it, he felt his heart
lurch and race beneath his ribs.

8. Beset by fears, she became
the hare who hears
the mowers' voices growing louder.

HASENKALENDER
für *Valerie Gillies*

1. Am nasskalten Ende des Winters
ist der Berg halb Schnee, halb
blasses Gras. Nur wenn der Schnee
sich bewegt, wird er zum Hasen.

2. Schaffst du es, einen Hasen zu fangen
und ihm in die Augen zu schauen
siehst du die ganze Welt.

3. An dem Tag im März
als sie zwei Hasen am Feldrand
beim Boxen sah
strampelte das Kind zum ersten Mal in ihr.

4. Sicher ist, Midas hat nie einen Hasen gesehen
sonst hätte ihn Gold nicht geblendet.

5. Wenn weit oben der Bussard kreist
wie ein langsamer Drachen
lässt der Hase Schnur nach.

6. Behauptet jemand, er habe
an alles gedacht
hat er den Hasen vergessen.

7. Das Hasennest, warm aber leer.
Als er darüber stolperte, stockte
sein Herz unter den Rippen, raste.

8. Von Ängsten umzingelt, wurde sie
zum Hasen, der das Zischeln
der Sensen näher kommen hört.

9. Light as the moon's path over the sea,
the run of the hare over the land.

10. The birchwood a dapple
of fallen gold: a carved hare
lies in a Pictish hoard.

11. Waking to the cry of a hare
she ran and found the child sleeping.

12. November stiffens
into December: hare and grass
have grown a thick coat of frost.

9. Leicht wie der Mondstrahl über dem Wasser:
der Lauf eines Hasen übers Land

10. Der Birkenwald ein Flackern
aus Blattgold: bewegungslos
ein Hase, Statue aus einem piktischen Schatz.

11. Sie erwachte vom Schrei eines Hasen
stürzte zu ihrem Kind, es schlief.

12. November erstarrt
im Dezember: Hase und Gras
tragen einen Mantel aus Frost.

A SHEPHERD'S VOICE

(after 2 pictographic clay tablets from Tell Brak, Syria, c. 4000 BCE)

The river the clay was dug from
has vanished, so we must imagine

ducks squabbling
among the rushes, the flight

of cranes at sunset, night
erupting with bull-frog cries.

What's scratched into the clay
is a voice, a shepherd's, who declares

– Here are 10 goats
– Here are 10 sheep

His dry receipts remain
to tell us that barren desert

was pasture, watered, green;
and though his flocks have shrunk

to two baked bits of clay,
what's scratched there is

the shepherd's voice, calling
his beasts into our field of vision –

some lop-eared with rough brown coats,
others whose big horns coil like rope:

– Here are 10 goats
– Here are 10 sheep

coming to drink, bells clunking, sending up
bird-cries; the reeds confer, the water laps.

STIMME EINES SCHÄFERS

(nach 2 Tontafeln mit Piktogrammen aus Tell Brak, Syrien, ca. 4000 v. Chr.)

Der Fluss, aus dem der Ton gewonnen wurde,
ist verschwunden, wir müssen uns also

vorstellen: kabbelnde Enten im Schilf,
den Flug der Kraniche abends, die Nacht

die mit dem Krawall
der Frösche hervorbricht.

In den Ton gekratzt eine Stimme,
die Stimme eines Schäfers, der erklärt:

– *Das hier sind 10 Ziegen*
– *Das hier sind 10 Schafe*

Trockene Belege, aber sie überdauern,
erinnern uns daran, dass Wüste

Weide war, bewässert, grün.
Die Herden sind geschrumpft

zu zwei Stück gebranntem Ton
doch in den Ton gekratzt

die Stimme des Schäfers, sie ruft
seine Tiere uns ins Bewusstsein –

Hängeohren, raues, braunes Fell
Hörner, eingedreht wie Seile:

– *Das hier sind 10 Ziegen*
– *Das hier sind 10 Schafe*

Sie kommen zur Tränke mit klimpernden Glocken, lassen
Vogelrufe auffliegen. Schilf wispert, Wasser schwappt.

ANNA CROWE

MENDED FENCE, BARRA

after a photograph by John Cooper

> Let no smalnesse retard thee; if thou beest not a Cedar to help
> towards a palace, if thou beest not Amber, Bezoar nor liquid gold,
> to restore Princes; yet thou art a shrub to shelter a lambe, or to
> feed a bird; or a plantane to ease a child's smart, or a grasse to
> cure a sick dog.
>
> John Donne, *Essays in Divinity*

Darned like the heel of a sock, like boot-hose,
with baler's twine instead of worsted, with rope
and string and twists of wire, the mended fence
reveals itself as a kind of random knitting.
Purely utilitarian, this link-work
has a beauty that's all pro tem, ad hoc,
with textures suggestive of the wider picture,
differences: a study in tensions where
the braced immutability of the post,
split and splintered, poker-worked
by shadows of staple-ring and hook,
is relished no less than the angled span
of iron rails as flat as swords, pocked
and grizzled, and buttoned by rivets: and if a line
of galvanised steel opens its arms
like a horizon after rain, or if it receives
the downward skewering twist of wire
that feathers the light like a gannet,
it's accidental; and there is still room
for twine and string, each with its proper weight
and implicated strength, to be roped-in.
Nylon twine radiates sun, fraying,
and ends of string are wanton tassels of frizz,
but this small net of knots and hitches, reefs
and grannies, deters the straying lamb and plays
cat's cradle with the wind as it lingers or passes,

GEFLICKTER ZAUN AUF BARRA

nach einer Fotografie von John Cooper

> Lass dich von Größe nicht beeindrucken; Du musst keine Zeder sein, die
> den Palast ermöglicht, kein Bernstein, Bezoarstein oder flüssiges Gold, um
> Prinzen zu heilen; Du kannst ein Busch sein zur Herberge für das Lamm
> und Festmahl für den Vogel, oder ein Wegerich, der den Schmerz des Kindes
> lindert, oder auch Gras, das den kranken Hund heilt.
>
> *John Donne, Essays in Divinity*

Wie eine Strumpfferse gestopft, oder Fischersocken,
mit Bindegarn statt Kammgarn, mit Strippe,
Strick, verdrehtem Draht, ist der geflickte
Zaun eine Art Zufallshäkeln. Purer
Nutzen, Flechtwerk, und seine Schönheit
ganz ad hoc, pro tem, Texturen die aufs
Gesamtbild deuten, auf Kontrast: eine Studie
über Spannung, in der die störrische Konstanz
des Pfostens, der zerspalten und zersplittert ist,
gebrandmalt vom Schatten der Krampen
und Haken, nicht weniger Gefallen findet,
als die langgestreckten, sich kreuzenden
Stangen, flach wie Schwerter, narbig,
gesprenkelt und nietengeknöpft: Wenn eine Linie
aus verzinktem Stahl ihre Arme ausbreitet
wie ein Horizont nach dem Regen, oder wenn sie
die Abwärtsdrehung des Drahts annimmt,
die das Licht auffächert wie ein Basstölpel
im Sturzflug, dann nur aus Zufall; und es gibt
immer Gelegenheit für Garn und Faser,
durchs eigene Gewicht und gehaspelte
Kraft verwickelt zu werden. Nylonschnur
strahlt Sonne aus, franst, und Faden-
enden sind flausige zerzauste Quasten,
aber dieses kleine Netz aus Knoten und Schlägen,
aus Schotstek und Reffstich schreckt streunende

muttering (to a droned continuo
of shepherd's thyme and turf and gorse, sheep's dung,
sea-weed, diesel) snatches of things like

>   *if thou beest not a Cedar*
>   and
> *no man is an island*
>   and
>   *make do and mend.*

Lämmer und spielt das Fadenspiel mit dem Wind,
der still hält oder davontreibt und raunt
(zu einem dröhnenden Continuo aus Quendel
Torf und Ginster, Schafsdung, Diesel, Tang)
Fetzen von etwas wie

if thou beest not a Cedar

oder

no man is an island

oder

aus alt mach neu.

ANNA CROWE

SARI

for Christopher and Daphne

Four thousand miles from Scotland, we're at home
among the rainy mountains, the fields of leeks
and cabbages, the hills that promise tea.
The train clattered and drummed like the Kandyan
dancers at your wedding, blowing its horn
like the conch that brings the bride to the *Poruwa*.

Those cakes of milky rice you fed each other
swelled and sweetened into days you shared
with us. And now you're hammering at our door
in the *Ella Grand Motel* to tell us that dawn
is the time to see the most amazing view
in the world. *Christopher's waking us up again!*

your father groans – the way you'd prise open
our eyelids, sharing your every moment, or just
a wee boy scared to go for a pee in the dark.
But all your life you've been opening our eyes,
and now you've tiptoed away from your sleeping wife
to coax us over the dew to the edge, to show us

Ella's famous *Gap*: the light is grey
up here in the grassy gods, the wings dark,
but from six thousand feet we can look through
as the play begins, and day unfolds itself
like the sari a man must wrap around his bride.
A sea of rose-gold pearl whose wave-crests

SARI

für Christopher und Daphne

Viertausend Meilen von Schottland entfernt fühlen wir uns
zuhause zwischen verregneten Bergen, Feldern
mit Porree und Kohl, Hängen, die Tee versprechen.
Der Zug klopft und trommelt wie die Kandy-
Tänzer bei eurer Hochzeit, sein Horn tönt
wie das Muschelhorn, das die Braut zum *Poruwa* ruft.

Der Kuchen aus milchigem Reis, mit dem ihr euch füttert
geht auf und süßt die Tage, die ihr mit uns teilt. Und nun
hämmerst du an unsere Tür im *Grand Ella Motel,*
um uns zu sagen, dass sich bei Dämmerung
der unglaublichste Blick der Welt
auftut. *Christopher weckt uns mal wieder!*

stöhnt dein Vater – die Art, wie du unsere Augenlider
anhobst, um uns etwas Wichtiges mitzuteilen, oder einfach
ein winziger Kerl, der Angst hatte, im Dunkeln pinkeln zu gehen.
Dein ganzes Leben schon hast du uns die Augen geöffnet,
und jetzt hast du dich leise von deiner schlafenden Frau entfernt,
um uns über den Tau an den Rand des Tals zu locken und uns Ellas

berühmtes *Gap* zu zeigen: Das Licht ist grau hier oben
auf unserer grasigen Galerie, die Kulissen noch dunkel,
aber von sechstausend Fuß Höhe aus erhaschen wir
einen Blick darauf, als das Stück beginnt und der Tag sich entfaltet
wie der Sari, den ein Bräutigam um seine Braut wickelt.
Rosa-goldenes Perlmuttmeer, die Wellenkämme

are mountains as far as the horizon; peaks
appearing, sharpening as the bowl fills up
with milk. A hundred miles away, a lake
opens its eye, and though our hanging valley's
dark, the sky is slowly whitening;
a bird tries out its xylophone of notes,

rippling up the octave towards the moment
when a tree in the wings will suddenly glitter,
and colour flood the hill and wash us home
on a tide of waterfalls and spice and sweat
to Colombo, London, Fife; into the world
and all that patterned life we can't yet see.

bis zum Horizont sind Berge; Gipfel tauchen auf,
ihre Umrisse immer deutlicher, während die Schüssel
sich mit Milch füllt. Hundert Meilen entfernt öffnet
ein See die Augen, unser hängendes Tal
immer noch dunkel, der Himmel schon heller;
ein Vogel probiert sein Xylophon aus Tönen aus,

plätschert eine Oktave hoch zu dem Moment,
in dem ein Baum in den Kulissen plötzlich glitzert
und Farbe die Hänge überschwemmt, uns heimwärts
spült mit einer Flut aus Wasserfällen, Gewürzen, Süße,
nach Colombo, London, Fife: in die Welt und das bunt
gemusterte Leben, das wir noch nicht sehen.

ODILE KENNEL }

interpreter }
Sprachmittlerin }

{ **ANNA CROWE**

{ Katy Derbyshire

ODILE KENNEL

WENN ICH DIE AUGEN SCHLIESSE, IST DER HIMMEL EIN BAGGER

gelb, seine Schaufel so groß
dass die Welt hineinpasst. Er ist der Gott
aller Bagger auf Erden. Ihn beten sie an
mit jedem Klackklack ihrer Gelenke
ihr chorisches Wühlen ist ein Wüten
gegen ihre *conditio technica*, ihr Jaulen
im Tosen der Baustellen ein Jauchzen
Obertonsingen für göttliche Ohren.
Im Gleichtakt recken sie ihre Greifer
zum Himmel empor, doch diesen Takt
nähme man nur von dort oben aus wahr
wenn man selbst Gott wäre, Himmel oder
ein Bagger in der Größe des Himmels.
(Vielleicht ahnen Kinder die Nöte
der Bagger oder sie wollen Gott sein
der die Schaufeln bedient.) Ich öffne
die Augen, der Himmel ist eine riesige
Schaufel, gelb, hängt
am Gelenk des Alls.

nach einer Zeile von Carl-Christian Elze

WHEN I CLOSE MY EYES THE SKY IS A DIGGER

yellow, its shovel so big
that the world fits in. It's the god
of all diggers on earth. This is the one they pray to
with every clack-clack of their joints
their choral hacking out is a raging
against their conditio technica, their groaning
in the roar of the building sites a jubilant
singing with overtones for divine ears.
Straining in unison, their claws
implore the heavens, yet this rhythm
would be perceptible only from above
if you yourself were god, heaven
or a digger the size of the sky.
(Perhaps children sense the diggers' angst
or they want to be god,
operating the shovels.) I open
my eyes, and the sky is a huge
shovel, yellow, dangling
from the joint of the world.

after a line by Carl-Christian Elze

ODILE KENNEL

IM HOF DER TSCHATSCHENDEN FRISÖRE

> Frisöre verlangen ihre ganz eigene
> literarische Herangehensweise.
> *Felicitas Hoppe*

> Les coiffeurs demandent
> une approche littéraire particulière.
> *Emmanuelle Pagano*

immer träume ich von blauen
Kletterschuhen und einem Hof
voller Frisöre. Die Frisöre
rauchen, es sind viele, und sie reden
von Haaren. Dank der blauen Schuhe
gelange ich hinunter in den Hof
ich setze mich zu den Frisören
und rauche mit ihnen. Rauche
schweigend, weil ich nichts
über Haare zu sagen habe.
Sie rufen Rapunzel und meinen
nicht mich. Und weil Rapunzel
jemand anderes ist und hier
nicht wohnt, weiß ich nicht
wie ich zurück nach oben komme.
Die Frisöre fragen, was bedeutet
tschatschen, ich antworte:
tchatcher, ihr coiffeure!
Kennt ihr das nicht? Jeden Morgen
werde ich wach davon und weiß jetzt
es geht um Haare, was hatte ich
anderes erwartet? Sie ziehn
an ihren Kippen, ich kipple
auf meinem Stuhl, frage mich
und die Frisöre, was Sigmund
sagen würde zu meinen

IN THE CHATCHING HAIRDRESSERS' BACKYARD

Hairdressers demand their very own
literary approach
Felicitas Hoppe

Les coiffeurs demandent
une approche littéraire particulière
Emmanuelle Pagano

I'm always dreaming of blue
climbing shoes and a backyard
full of hairdressers. The hairdressers,
lots of them, smoke, and they talk
about hair. Thanks to the blue shoes
I climb down into the yard
I sit with the hairdressers
and smoke with them. Smoke
in silence, because I have nothing
to say about hair.
Rapunzel, they call and don't
mean me. And because Rapunzel
is someone else and doesn't
live here, I don't know
how I'll get back up.
The hairdressers ask, What does
chatching mean? I answer:
tchatcher, you *coiffeurs!*
Don't you know? Every morning
it wakes me up and now I find
it's about hair, what on earth
did I expect? They puff
on their fags, I shuffle
my chair, ask myself
and the hairdressers what Sigmund
would say about my

Kletterschuhen, warum
sind sie blau, und was
ist der Sinn von Frisören.
Doch die Frisöre hören
nicht zu, die Frisöre
gehen zurück an die Arbeit.
Und ich, ich sitze im Hof
wie ein nasser Hund

climbing shoes – why
are they blue, and what
is the meaning of hairdressers.
But the hairdressers don't
listen, the hairdressers
go back to work.
As for me, I sit in the yard
like a wet dog

TIERE ZU FRAGEN

Fragen zu Tieren
und Tiere zu Fragen
zu Flugscharen von
schartigen Schaben
Schabernack treibenden
Staren, treiben
windige Winzlinge
ins Auge oder sind das
Flusen, Pudelmuster
auf Blusen, schon
wummern Hufe
an Schläfen, zähl
Schäfchen, zähl
wolliges Dasein
auf Deichen, in Teichen
Schalenweichtiere
und Schnabeltiereier
im Lolch, Molche
besing, besing solche
die schweigen, Zwei-
seitentiere, weiche
Korallen, und Quallen
vergiss nicht, die
auch Durst haben
Mondfische, Woll-
schweine, eigentliche
Eulen, Chako-Pekaris
Okapis, Gorgonen
polternde Drohnen
und jetzt die Fragen:

BESTIAL QUESTIONS

questions on animals
and animals on quests
for festering nests
of gestating cockroaches
hoaching, encroaching
on rockhopper penguins
grasshopping dingoes
that sing to the moon
crooning to spoonbills
while oodles of poodles
go paddling for ducks
pluckily swimming
on seersucker lakes
to peer for, speir for
a stuffed duckbilled platypus
flatfish and krill
and rough stolonifera
that grow upon pylons
high on the prairie
where buffalo graze
praise them, O praise them
these quiet conchifera
top-shells, clams, ammonites
do not neglect them
the newts, nerds and nerkles
ladybirds, thirsty ones
ticks, crickets, midges
linnets and peewits
true owls and quails
false birds of paradise
peccaries, okapis
plump anacondas
and bumbling drones
and now for the questions:

NACH PASÁRGADA

aus dem Fenster schauen, sich vergewissern
dass man existiert, weil die Welt
da draußen existiert. Drinnen
sind Bücher, vielleicht der Gedanke
an ein Kind, das man nie hatte, ist
ein Bett, eine Schreibmaschine.
Ein Telefon, das klingelt, wiederum
Welt nachweist, Töne, elektrische
Signale. Dann hinaus, gehen
durch die Stadt. Die kein Beweis ist
dass es das Drinnen gibt hinter
den Fensterläden, schon eher
der Milchmann, der Zeitungsverkäufer:
Aufblitzen einer Möglichkeit, Falten
im Anzug, Gesten des Alltags,
die Rettung der Substantive
Radfahren, Könige, Lektionen
vom Weggehen, jedes Ding
an seinem Platz

Nach dem Film »O poeta do castelo« über Manuel Bandeira
von Joaquim Pedro de Andrade (1959)

GOING TO PASÁRGADA

looking out of the window, reassuring yourself
that you exist, because the world
outside exists. Inside
there are books, perhaps the thought
of a child you never had,
a bed, a typewriter.
A telephone that rings, evidence
in its turn of world, sounds, electric
signals. Then out, walking
through the city. Which is no evidence
that the inside exists behind
shutters, though more probable
are the milkman, the newspaper seller:
the flash of a possibility, creases
in your suit, everyday gestures,
the rescuing of the nouns
bicycles, kings, lessons
in leaving, each thing
in its place

after the film "O poeta do castelo" about Manuel Bandeira
by Joaquim Pedro de Andrade (1959)

DIE METAPHORISCHE LOGIK EINER VERBINDUNG

es gibt keinen Beweis, dass wir
gemeinsam hier einkehrten. Nicht einmal
die hellen Rechtecke am Hang, die Horizont
von hinter der Berglinie in den Himmel
hieven, in Wirklichkeit aber die hellen
Stellen spiegeln in mir, sind ein Beweis
für die Herkunft der hellen Stellen.

Oder doch Fenster in meinem Körper
der ein Hang ist, um die Stadt drapiert
Tal bildet, das der metaphorischen
Logik nach du wärst, jeder könnte in uns
einkehren, wir wären durch Straßen, Parks
Trottoirs verbunden (und durch ein *a*)

ah, und ein Fluss flösse durch die Stadt
mit Brücken und Schiffen, schon allein
der Metaphern wegen. Und am Ufer
stünden Kinder und winkten, aber das

ist schon eine andere Stadt, durch die
wir trieben, auch hier keine Beweise
nicht einmal das zersprengte
Licht über dem Wasser, das in Wirklichkeit
die trudelnden Tupfer spiegelt in mir
oder ist mein Körper ein Fluss, such
dir aus, was du der metaphorischen Logik
nach wärst (etwas mit u?) oder ich
oder du oder

ODILE KENNEL | ANNA CROWE

THE METAPHORICAL LOGIC OF A CONNECTION

there is no proof that we
swept in here together. Not even
the bright squares of the steep streets, that shoulder
horizon from behind the line of mountains into the
sky in reality however reflecting the bright
spots inside of me, are a proof
of the origin of the bright spots.

Or actually the window in my body,
which is steep streets, draped around the town
forms a deep cleft, which in metaphorical
logic would be you, anyone could sweep into
us, we'd be connected by streets, parks
trottoirs (and by an *é*)

yes, and a river would flow through the town
with bridges and boats, simply
for the sake of the metaphors. And on the banks
children would stand and wave, but that

is another town through which
we once drifted, with no proof here either
not even the shattered
light upon the water, which in reality
reflects the whirling dots inside me
or is my body a river, you choose
what you'd be, according to the metaphorical logic
(something beginning with *i*) or I
or you or

ANNA CROWE

The week spent working with Odile Kennel and Katy Derbyshire in Berlin was one of the most pleasurable weeks in my entire life. I thought how naming the project VERSschmuggel (meaning smuggling verses) had been a stroke of genius – lending our endeavours an illicit, conspiratorial sense of working in secret to carry something marvellous across frontiers and against the odds. Juliane Henrich was filming us while we talked, questioned, sang, laughed, but so unobtrusive was she that we forgot her presence. Looking for an image to describe the dynamic of how we worked – listening, testing the weight of a word or phrase, building the translation (and how fortunate we were in having the incomparable Katy to help and suggest, and in having French as a third language to provide checks and balances) – I thought of the Catalan castellers building their human castles in Alexanderplatz below our window, an image of daring, trust, and balance, climbing, sustaining each other with linked hands.

ODILE KENNEL

Hinter Gedichten stehen Geschichten, hinter übersetzten Gedichten auch. Wir suchten Tiere, fragten nach Nerds: Sind das nicht kleine, fellige Wesen? If I ran the zoo, sagt Dr. Seuss, und er fügte dem Zoo neue Tiere hinzu: A Nerkle, a Nerd, and a Seersucker, too. Wären wir Seeleute, wir würden die Namen der Knoten kennen, wir wüssten, wie man sie löst: How are we going to get out of these verses? Wir fanden hinaus, entwirrten Knäuel und Knoten, verwirrend schnell, ja, hatte da nicht jemand seine Zauberhand im Spiel? Wir spielten und spielten auf: Kinderlieder, Volkslieder, Popsongs, und zur Illustration des Wortes Jauchzen das Bachsche Weihnachtsoratorium. Anna kannte zu jedem Stichwort ein Lied. Draußen herrschten 35 °C , Katalanen bauten Menschenpyramiden auf dem Alexanderplatz und forderten Katalonien will wählen. Wie Schottland gewählt hat, wissen wir, ich meinerseits habe längst Schottland gewählt nach diesen drei Tagen mit Anna Crowe und Katy Derbyshire, in denen wir die Geschichten hinter den Gedichten erzählten und die Geschichten hinter den übersetzten Gedichten erzählend erschufen: Im klimatisierten Paradies, dixit Katy, hatten wir es gut!

ANNA CROWE

Die Woche, in der ich mit Odile Kennel und Katy Derbyshire in Berlin zusammengearbeitet habe, war eine der schönsten in meinem ganzen Leben. Mir fiel auf, was für ein Geniestreich es bedeutet hatte, das Projekt *VERSschmuggel* zu nennen – unsere Anstrengungen bekamen damit einen verbotenen, konspiratorischen Charakter; im Geheimen arbeitend und alle Hindernisse überwindend, brachten wir etwas Wunderbares über die Grenze. Juliane Heinrich filmte uns dabei, während wir redeten, fragten, sangen, lachten. Sie tat das so unaufdringlich, dass wir ihre Anwesenheit gar nicht mehr wahrnahmen. Wenn ich nach einem Bild suche für die Dynamik, in der wir zusammenarbeiteten – also zuhörten, das Gewicht eines Wortes oder Satzes prüften, die Übersetzung zusammentrugen (und was für ein Glück wir hatten, dass die unvergleichliche Katy uns zur Seite stand und Vorschläge machte, und dass wir das Französische als dritte Sprache und weiteren Prüfstein heranziehen konnten) – fallen mir die katalanischen *castellers* ein, die unter unserem Fenster am Alexanderplatz ihre Menschenpyramiden bauten, ein Bild des Wagemuts, des Vertrauens und Gleichgewichts, kletternd, einander die Hände reichend und sich gegenseitig stützend.

ODILE KENNEL

Behind poems there are stories, and behind translated poems as well. We sought out animals, asked after nerds: aren't they small, furry creatures? *If I ran the zoo*, says Dr. Seuss, he'd add to the zoo some animals too: *A Nerkle, a Nerd and a Seersucker, too.* Were we sailors, we'd know the names of knots, we'd know how to undo them. *How are we going to get out of these verses?* We did find the way out, unscrambled puzzles and knots with puzzling speed; and it certainly seemed that someone had a magic hand in that. We hammed it up playing nursery rhymes, folk songs, pop songs, and to elluci-date the word *Jauchzen* (rejoice, cheer), we played Bach's Christmas Oratorium. Anna knew a song for every keyword. Outside, it was 35°C, Catalans were building human pyramids on Alexanderplatz and demanded: *Catalonia wants to choose.* We know now, what Scotland chose. For my part though, I chose Scotland a long time ago, after those three days with Anna Crowe and Katy Derbyshire, by telling the stories behind the poems and in telling them, creating the stories behind the translated poems: in the air-conditioned paradise, dixit Katy, we had it made in the shade!

ROBIN ROBERTSON 　}

interpreter 　}
Sprachmittler 　}

{ ULRIKE DRAESNER

{ Tom Morrison

ROBIN ROBERTSON

ANNUNCIATION
after Fra Angelico

He has come from the garden, leaving
no shadow, no footprint in the dew.
They hold each other's gaze at the point
of balance: everything streaming
towards this moment, streaming away.

A word will set the seed
of life and death,
the over-shadowing of this girl
by a feathered dark.
But not yet: not quite yet.

How will she remember the silence
of that endless moment?
Or the end, when it all began –
the first of seven joys
before the seven sorrows?

She will remember the aftersong
because she is only human.
One day
she'll wake with wings, or wake
and find them gone.

VERKÜNDIGUNG
nach Fra Angelico

Gekommen ist er durch den Garten, kein
Schatten fiel, kein Fuß auf Tau.
Achsen kreuzen ihre Blicke, Linien
Schwebe: alles strömt zu
diesem Augenblick, strömt fort von ihm.

Ein Wort wird den Samen ausbringen
für Leben und Tod,
die gefiederte Dunkelheit, die auch dieses
Mädchen überschatten will.
Doch nicht jetzt: nicht schon jetzt.

Wie wird sie sich an die Stille
dieses unendlichen Augenblickes erinnern?
Oder an das Ende, als alles seinen Anfang nahm –
die erste der sieben Freuden
vor den sieben Schmerzen?

Sie wird sich erinnern an das Lied nach dem Lied
ist sie doch nicht mehr als ein Menschenkind.
Eines Tages
wird sie mit Flügeln erwachen, wird erwachen
und finden, dass sie verloren sind.

THE FISHERMEN'S FAREWELL

Their long stares mark them apart; eyes gone
to sea-colours: grey, foam-flecked

and black in the undertow, blue
as the blue banners of the mackerel, whipping west.

On land, they are smoke-walkers, where each stone
is a standing stone, every circle a stone circle.

They would be rumour if they could, in this frozen
landscape like a stopped sea, from the great stone keels

of Callanish to the walls of Dunnottar and Drum.
They would be less even than rumour:

to be ocean-stealers, to never throw a shadow –
to dream the blank horizon and dread the sight of land.

The drink storms through these men, uncompasses
them, till they're all at sea again.

Their houses, heeled over in the sand:
each ruin now a cairn for kites.

And down by the quay
past empty pots, unmended nets and boats:

this tiny bar, where men sleep upright
in their own element, as seals.

DIE AUSFAHRT DER FISCHER

Ihr in die Weite gerichtetes Starren sondert sie ab; in ihren Augen
spielen die Farben der See: grau, schaumgesprenkelt

schwarz unterströmt, blau
wie die blauen Banner der Makrelenschule, blitzende Schläge westwärts.

An Land sind sie Schall und Rauch, wo jeder Stein
ein Hinkelstein ist, jeder Kreis ein Steinkreis.

Wünschten sie wären, könnten sie nur, nichts als Gerücht, in dieser gefrorenen
Landschaft, diesem erstarrten Meer von den großen Steinkielen

von Callanish bis zu den Bollwerken von Dunnottar und Drum.
Wünschten sie wären weniger noch als Gerücht:

wollten Ozeandiebe sein, niemals einen Schatten werfen –
den Horizont leer träumen, tilgen alles Land.

Der Schnaps stürmt durch die Männer, lässt ihre Kompassnadel rotieren
bis samt und sonders sie wieder taumeln auf hoher See.

Ihre Häuser kippen kopfüber in den Sand:
jeder Schotterhaufen jetzt ein Steinmal für Milane.

Und unten an der Mole
hinter leeren Körben, ungeflickten Netzen und Booten:

der kleine Ausschank, wo Männer im Stehen schlafen
ganz in ihrem Element, wie Robben.

THE SHELTER

I should never have stayed here
in this cold shieling
once the storm passed
and the rain had finally eased.

I could make out shapes
inside, the occasional sound:
a muffled crying
which I took for wind in the trees;
a wasp,
stuttering there at the windowsill.
I listened. What looked like
a small red coat
was dripping from its wire hanger.

There was a shift and rustle
coming from the bucket in the corner
by the door; I found, inside,
a crumpled fist of balled-up paper, slowly
uncrinkling.

On the hearth, just legible
in the warm ash, my name and dates,
and above that, in a shard
of mirror left in the frame,
I caught sight of myself, wearing
something like a black brooch at the neck.
Then I looked more closely
and saw what it was.

OBDACH

Ich hätte hier auf keinen Fall bleiben sollen
in dieser kalten Schutzhütte
als der Sturm sich endlich legte
und der Regen nachließ zuletzt.

Ich konnte Formen
im Inneren ausmachen, ab und an einen Laut:
ein gedämpftes Weinen
das ich für ein Wehen in den Bäumen hielt;
eine Wespe
stotternd da am Fensterbrett.
Ich lauschte. Etwas, das aussah wie
ein kleiner roter Mantel
tropfte vom Drahtbügel.

Bewegung, Geraschel
aus dem Eimer in der Ecke
nahe der Tür; ich fand in ihm
eine geballte Faust zusammengeknüllten Papiers, die sich
langsam entknitterte.

Auf der Feuerstelle, eben noch lesbar
in der nachglühenden Asche, mein Name und meine Lebensdaten
und darüber, in einer Spiegelscherbe
die noch im Rahmen hing,
geriet ich mir selbst in den Blick
etwas wie eine schwarze Brosche am Hals.
Ich fasste es schärfer ins Auge
und begriff, was es war.

ROBIN ROBERTSON

GLASS OF WATER AND COFFEE POT
after Chardin

These rooms of wood, of tongue-and-groove, open out
on a garden of white-washed walls and a maple tree,
a new Spring bright among the weathered stone and brick.
We find things that are old and used, well-made, well worn
and beautiful because of this. The balance
intimate between that glass of water's clarity and light
and the pot's grave darkness: an order so luminous
and fine you needn't measure it with a rule, just look.
The papery whiteness of the garlic heads is the same light
held in the water glass, the same light lifting a gleam
from the blackened coffee pot that's somehow managed
to make it through, to find harmony here
on this stone shelf, happiness of the hand and heart,
to keep its heat and still pour clean and true.

WASSERGLAS MIT KAFFEEKANNE
nach Chardin

Diese Räume aus Holz, verbunden durch Feder und Nut, öffnen sich
auf einen Garten mit gekalkten Mauern und einem Ahorn
einen frischen Frühling, schimmernd zwischen verwitterten Ziegeln und Stein.
Wir finden Dinge, alt und gebraucht, so kundig gemacht wie genutzt
und darum schön. Der innige Gleichklang
zwischen diesem Glas von Wasserklarheit, Wasserlicht
und der ernsten Dunkelheit der Kanne: eine ebenso feine
wie aus sich selbst leuchtende Anordnung
die kein Lineal je ausmisst, die nur das Auge sieht.
Das papierne Weiß der Knoblauchknollen ist von demselben Licht
wie das Wasser im Glas, demselben Licht, das diesen Schimmer
aus der geschwärzten Kaffeekanne entbindet, der es auf welchen Wegen
auch immer gelungen ist, noch da zu sein, und sie hier zu finden, die Harmonie
auf dem Steinregal, das Glück der Hand und des Herzens
die Hitze zu halten und bis heute sauber und genau auszuschenken.

ULRIKE DRAESNER

interpreter
Sprachmittler

{ ROBIN ROBERTSON

{ Tom Morrison

CHLOROPHYLL

diese schulstunde blieb, ihr agent
lautlos, ihr könig: das blatt
frisst licht macht zucker ohne
unterlass schlich darauf ich
durch **sonnenfutterschein** nach haus
zwischen bäumen stauden gras
roh an unsichtbare zitzen licht gesaugt

auf der zunge das brechende blatt
das füllwort »grün« für phyl
deine augen, mittags, im schilf
bei flötenapp, bei offner autotür
intimmodul auf gras: einander zärtlich
ein wenig ohne lügen zu liegen
versucht einander grün

in licht das fiel sich drehte wehrte
bis zucker wuchs das füllwort
»fühl« bei offner autotür
nach flötenapp ging ich allein
nach haus einen fleck im rock
von gras gesaugt so tief dass
jedes licht darüber lief

CHLOROPHYLL

The school lesson stayed with me;
its secret king, the leaf, eats the light,
makes sugar unrelentingly;
I slipped home, then, through the sun-foddered light
between trees, shrubs, grass,
being drawn up rough
to the light's invisible teats.

On my tongue the breaking leaf, the filler-word 'green'
for *phyll*; your eyes, at noon in the reeds
accompanied by Pan's reed-pipe
piped through the opened car door to the two of us
mechanically at work in the grass,
our last attempt to lie together
without lying, to be green to each other again.

In light that fell, turned, resisted,
until sugar grew like the filler-word
'feel' and I left you there:
with the car door open, and the pipes:
the grass stain drawn
so deep into my skirt, so green,
that all the light ran off it.

SCHÖNEWEIDE, SCHÖNEWEIDE

heute werden die frösche einst prinzliche
wurfgeschosse in den tiefen des lebens
gelöst manche sagen die tiefe sei einfach
ein keller dunkel ein wenig feucht sie
kleben versteht sich in diesem sinn:
abgemacht.
schöneweide schöneweide

sie zieht den mund sich weit dem kind
die spange von den zähnen: »beiß
in diesen haufen reis!« ab sofort patschhände
patch ist der cent nach dem simultan
man sich bückt kupferdraht
            schöneweide schöneweide
kupferdraht

verwendung wand: brautkleid in fetzen
s-bahnscheiben sicht: stöckelschuh
auf kellerstrich fest sie zieht
den mund sich nach von der wand
unnachahmlich soft die frage rinnt
stimmchen kind: **zerhochtungsfest**, ihr
macht?
      schöneweide schöneweide
fahr

an der scheibe schlangenseite
verwendung wand: herz hand hirn ent-
hocht ein haufen reis
      schöneweide schöneweide

SCHÖNEWEIDE, SCHÖNEWEIDE

Today, the frogs – once princes
shot flat against the wall,
all this in the depths of life –
are unstuck; some say the depth is simply
a cellar, dark, a little damp, they stick,
but only in the sense of *being torn*.
Schöneweide, Schöneweide

I widen my mouth, drawing with the lipstick,
pull the brace from the child's teeth.
Bite into this mound of rice!
Chubby hands of a child, clapping.
Here, two bend for one coin,
stretched from both sides slowly into copper-wire.
                    Schöneweide, Schöneweide
copper-wire

Now let me tell you how to use a wall.
Wedding-dress in tatters,
staring out of the S-Bahn,
I see one high-heeled shoe
stuck fast on the cellar floor,
I re-touch my lipstick; from the wall
trickles the question, in its little voice:
'the **unmarrying** feast, can you make that word?'
                    Schöneweide, Schöneweide
go

Through the window, snake-side,
another way to use a wall: heart, hand, brain, all
coming down to earth; a pile of rice,
                    Schöneweide, Schöneweide

gestartet einst, gestaunt, gestaut
star am steig gestern noch gefleckt
die brust (irr tüpfel weiß) fetzen kleid
gestreut gestarrt »zu herzen
ging«: schlangenei die hügel
vor der scheibe schlangenhülse
»hab mich
lieb«

im keller batterienkraft wäsche frosch
kommodenbild am öltank schuh gestellt
gewärmt gehöhlt kind – beeil dich –
gemacht (jeder weiß wie *das* sich liegt)
        schöneweide schöneweide
fahr

folie auf dem s-bahnfenster (»hab mich
verliebt«): nachts auf offnem wagen decke
bis zum kinn gestarrt als junge frau
als regen kam blitzend unter plane
sterne nach: himmelsreis, ihm und
ihr zuhauf

festgenagelt (mit der zunge an die wand)
zusammenziehen um zu sparen (wuhle
eiche grüne trift) im brautkleid s-bahn
fuhr verhielten jäger im hochsitz
sich die himmel wolken jokerlich
schöneweide schöneweide
alles vor ihr-ihm als »wir« und
keiner da

Long ago we started – startled, sticky – yesterday,
like the starling on the slope, my own breast
was still starred (crazy white dots), the tattered dress,
scattered, gaze frozen. *It went to the heart.*
The hills outside the window
look like snake eggs.
A snake's shed skin: the phrase: *Love me,*
please

In the cellar: a lot of machinery, laundry, a frog,
the cupboard with its wedding photo, shoes
lined up against the oil tank – we made warmth,
we made a hollow for it, we made a child – hurry up
(everyone knows how to do *that*).
                    Schöneweide, Schöneweide
go

Transfers on the S-Bahn window (*I've fallen in love*):
one night on the haycart, blanket drawn to the chin,
staring up as a young woman
as the rain came; under the blanket, we could see
the lightning flashes of the stars.
These stars, the rice of heaven
in this pilgrimage to plenty.

Nailed down (my tongue to the wall)
we moved in together to save money
(foraging for acorns in a green drift).
In my wedding-dress on the S-Bahn,
the hunters didn't shoot from their positions
but hung fire, while heaven held out the Joker.
Schöneweide, Schöneweide
everything before me/him/us
and no one there.

kascheln gegangen (wie einst) eis
unterm aquafilm zerkratztes
gesicht das kind seinen pinguin
auf geliehenen schuhen
schiebt die ängstlichkeit
nachts zwischen ihn sie
            (mich)
                schöneweide schöneweide

streckten uns, steif im keller
echohexe jagt schuh zu schuh
(am hochzeitstag) hinterm kessel
hinter fehlern ich die steuerung
(heizsystem) nach oben riss
zwei pfeile rot gekrümmt aufeinander
zu REPEAT
schweineöde schweineöde
schub

elstern krähen amselfeld die alte
wie die frische brut klebrige rotte
letztjährige kraft an den sohlen
vorm tank wummernd das hirn –
gekaschelt gekuschelt gekuscht
sah wer die verquollenen augen
putzte im spiegel zähne sich
das bild sah wer das krustenlächeln
im glas das rostrote glänzen
der scham
schöneweide schöneweide
reissack, schweiß
verwendung wand

ULRIKE DRAESNER | ROBIN ROBERTSON

We went skiting about on the ice and,
through the slush, I saw a scored face: our child
pushed her toy penguin
on borrowed skates, pushing
all our anxieties
at night between us.
                    Schöneweide, Schöneweide

We did our best, stiff in the cellar,
the Witch of Echoes hunting from shoe to shoe
(on the wedding day) behind the tank,
behind mistakes, I lever up
the central-heating system:
two red arrows turned
towards each other
telling me to REPEAT
Swine divide us, Swine divide us
ignite

Magpies, crows, blackbird-field, the first
and second fledglings; the stickiness of rot,
of last year's strength
clarted in the soles of my shoes;
my brain throbbing in front of the tank
– the skating, the embracing, the shaking –
who would see the puffy eyes, who was it
cleaning her teeth in the mirror,
who was it with the crusty smile in the glass,
who would see the rust-red blaze of shame?
Schöneweide, Schöneweide
rice in bulk, bagged up;
another way to use a wall.

verbogene kerzen picknicktasche
angelehnt das kind quappenglas
durchgefärbt gebrannt auf dem schoß
die wedelalgen (ware, hautig)
mit dem goldenen
ball gespielt
schöneweide schöneweide
ganz bei sich
schwimmen lernt

kupferdraht.
keller geträumt geräumt
gebrochen sei die tiefe einfach
sagen manche abgemacht das
kesselherz süchtig wummert wimmert
klebt (musst glauben daran) fahren
silberne kanten schlitter
den himmel ab

hinaus
mit roller und rad
pumpe picknick muskelkraft
folienverklebt (ball gespielt)
die fenster der bahn: rehe
jäger lillyfee
       helm halb überm gesicht
zieht das kind an der gardine
(pferdewagen, ehe
dem) lacht und zieht
den mund mir weit den
trauermund mir ab

      schöneweide schöneweide
fahr

Bent candles. The child sitting back in her seat
with a jar in her lap: fired colour, full of tadpoles
and algae, drifting like skin.
The child played with the golden ball.
Schöneweide, Schöneweide
All by herself
she learnt how to swim.

copper-wire
The cellar cleared: broken,
wrong. Some say the depth
is simply *torn*.
The heart, this addicted machine,
still thumps, jumps – *believes in* –
those silver blades sliding, shearing
round the heavens.

Go –
with scooter and bike
and bicycle-pump, picnic, muscle-power,
covered by transfers
(one of us playing with a ball)
the windows of the train,
the deer, the hunters;
her Lillyfee
          helmet half-covering her face,
the child pulls the curtain
(of the horse-drawn cart,
once upon a time),
laughs and – with a lipstick –
paints a smile onto the face of her mother
and takes the other, the sad mouth, away.

          Schöneweide, Schöneweide
go

ROBIN ROBERTSON

It's always a pleasure to be in Berlin – and it was a pleasure once again in June 2014, working with Ulrike Draesner under the wise and gentle supervision of Tom Morrison. One thing I realised during the process, while being questioned closely about the original reasoning behind a poem, was how little of my poetry emerges from the rational mind. Tom died a few weeks later, so what work I did in the city is dedicated to him.

ULRIKE DRAESNER

Da sitzen wir zu dritt, Robin Robertson, Tom Morrison und ich. Ich habe zwei Jahre in England gelebt und sitze, wie ich bald höre und in Robin Robertsons Gedichten auch sehe, mit zwei Schotten da, am Alexanderplatz in Berlin, und es ist Sommer, und wir sitzen am Meer. Wir sitzen im schottischen Wind, schottische Geister fahren uns um die Nase, Toms Short Fingers, als Brot, keep us going, ebenso sein schottisch starker Tee. Tom, der gute Geist dieses Übersetzens, Tom, der zuhört, vorschlägt, dessen Augen blitzen – wenn wir eintauchen: in Robins Makrelenschwarm, flügelnd im Atlantik vor Schottlands Steinen, in das Leuchten der Sprache unter dem Spiegel des Wassers. Wenn sie uns gelingt, die Spiegelung der Schönheit »poem«, wenn wir Lücken wahren, Mehrdeutigkeiten erfinden und Lauten folgen im eigenen Muster, wenn es gelingt, das Abakus-Zauber-Schieben »wir übersetzen Poesie«. Fröhlich soll ich hier schreiben, schrieb man mir, und ich denke an die Tage im Juni 2014 mit Robin und Tom, der wenige Wochen später starb. Ich denke an seine Freude an und aus der Dichtkunst, die nichts wäre, wüsste und fühlte sie unsere Vergänglichkeit nicht, kennte sie nicht unsere Leben samt ihren Öffnungen, Lücken und Spalten, sänge sie nicht eben davon. So schreibe ich hier, tatsächlich froh, froh in deed and thought eingedenk dessen, wie wir arbeiteten und wohin wir reisten, sehe Tom Morrisons Gesicht und spüre, was er liebte, da, im Raum, da, in den Worten, sehe ihn sitzen, im Wind, am Meer.

ROBIN ROBERTSON

Es ist immer ein Vergnügen, in Berlin zu sein – und das war es auch diesmal, als ich im Juni 2014 mit Ulrike Draesner unter der weisen und sanften Aufsicht Tom Morrisons zusammenarbeitete. Als ich im Laufe des Übersetzungsprozesses versuchte, die Fragen nach den ursprünglichen Gedanken hinter meinen Gedichten zu beantworten, wurde mir klar, wie wenig meine Gedichte rationalen Überlegungen entspringen.
Wenige Wochen später starb Tom. So ist meine Arbeit in Berlin ihm gewidmet.

ULRIKE DRAESNER

We're sitting there, the three of us, Robin Robertson, Tom Morrison and I. I lived in England for two years, and I'm sitting, as I soon hear – and in Robin Robertson's poems, also see – with two Scots, at Alexanderplatz in Berlin, and it is summer and we are sitting by the sea. We're sitting in the Scottish wind, Scottish ghosts are floating about over our shoulders, Tom's short fingers as bread, *keeping us going*, likewise his strong Scottish tea. Tom, the heart and soul of this translation process, Tom, who listens, suggests, whose eyes twinkle – when we dip: into Robin's mackerel swarm, winging over the Atlantic before Scotland's stones, into the lustre of language under the water's mirrored surface. When we manage a reflection of the beauty that is a "poem", when we preserve gaps, invent ambiguities and pursue sounds in their own pattern, when we magically balance the abacus, 'we translate poetry'. I should write cheerfully, they told me, and I think about the days in June with Robin and Tom, who died just a few weeks later. I think of his love of poetry, which would be nothing if it didn't know and feel our transience, if it didn't know our lives with all their openings, gaps and fissures, if it didn't sing about them. So I am writing here, indeed happy, happy *in deed and thought*, recalling how we worked and to where we travelled; I see Tom Morrison's face and sense what he loved, there, in the room, there, in the words, I see him sitting, in the wind, by the sea.

J. O. MORGAN }

interpreter
Sprachmittlerin }

KATHARINA SCHULTENS

Isabel Cole

Take two small goats, one fine, one average.
Keep the one of better breeding pure. Allow it
cream instead of milk so that its coat is glossy,
full, so that its softened skin is without spot.
Bring it indoors on cold nights. Sing it to sleep.
Put the lesser beast to the hill; strengthen its gut
with coarse dry grass; let its hair grow tangled,
thick as thorn; fill its belly with young; prolong
its pain in removing its pre-weaned kids, so that
each day it aches to contain such presses of milk.
And then, at the perfect moment, kill the other:
the coddled, virginal, hand-reared animal; let it
live on in the bound spines of books; as gloves,
fine knitwear; in casseroles, pâté, hors d'œuvres.
Let its cousin continue unknowingly, just as before:
more kids, more milk, its small neat hoofprints
divergent, repeated, for ever and ever, where
change favours only the fortunate, not the most fit.

nimm zwei junge Ziegen, perfekt die eine, die andere Durchschnitt
und halte die aus der besseren Linie absolut rein. gib ihr
Sahne, keine Milch, dann glänzt ihr Fell und bleibt
voll, ihre weiche Haut ist fleckenlos.
in kalten Nächten lass sie rein. sing bis sie schläft.
indes lass die geringere im Feld, das grobe Gras
stärkt ihren Magen; lass ihr Fell verfilzen
zu Dornenranken, stopf ihr den Bauch mit Jungen, zieh ihren Schmerz
noch in die Länge, wenn du ihr die nicht entwöhnten Zicklein nimmst,
damit die Milchfülle ihr täglich fast die Euter platzen lässt.
und dann, wenn der Moment perfekt ist, bring die andre um,
die von Hand aufgezogene verwöhnte Jungfrau, lass sie
weiterleben als gebundnen Buchrücken, als Handschuhpaar,
als Feinstrick, Schmortopfeinlage, Pastete und hors d'œuvre.
die Cousine lass darüber ganz im Dunkeln, sie soll leben wie bisher:
mehr Junge, noch mehr Milch, ihre adrette kleine Hufspur
in jeder Wiederholung divergierend, bis in alle Ewigkeit, dort wo
der Fortschritt nicht die Perfektion begünstigt, sondern die mit etwas Glück.

- I -

It's akin to a Venn diagram, where one circle is me
the other her, though that minor overlap is not
what we share, it represents our differences
colliding; the aspects of her world I must accept
in order to know her; the oddities of me she
must put up with just for us to speak. For if
we cannot manage even this then our circles
will un-lap, will be forced apart, to become again
two distinct circles, untouching and unknowable.

- II -

Similarly, the convergence of electron clouds;
those speeding near weightless particles that
hold mostly to their own set course, are content,
despite ionic tendencies to join, to make up the loss;
but, in joining, so they are changed, so they are
no longer themselves; their orbitals: shifted,
intermingled, made to flow around this
strange new composite, which, even in its fresh
stability, can still be broken, split into two
distinct bodies, adrift once more in the mix,
but active, quietly eager to make up the loss.

eventuell: ein Diagramm, ein Kreis bin ich,
der andre sie, aber die kleine Schnittmenge ist nicht
das, was wir teilen, sondern steht für unsre Differenzen,
dort, wo sie einander schneiden – die Aspekte ihres Lebens,
die ich, um sie zu kennen, akzeptieren muss; meine Eigenheiten,
mit denen sie sich abzufinden hat, allein, dass wir sprachfähig sind –
denn sollte uns nicht einmal das gelingen, werden unsre Kreise
sich voneinander lösen, auseinander treiben unter Zwang, erneut
zwei separate Kreise sein, voneinander unberührt und unerkannt einander.

ähnlich: Elektronenwolken, konvergierend;
in denen beinah schwerelose Teilchen rasen, die meist
auf ihrem selbst gesetzten Kurs bleiben, es genügt ihnen
– trotz ionischer Tendenz, sich zu verbinden – Mangel auszugleichen;
wenn sie sich aber binden, ändern sie ihr Selbst, sie sind
sie selbst nicht länger; ihre Bahnen sind verschoben,
kreisen nun um dieses merkwürdige neue Komposit,
das auch in seiner gerade erst erworbenen Stabilität
noch immer aufgebrochen werden kann, in zwei geteilt –
zwei Einzelkörper, die erneut in jener Wolke driften,
aktiviert: insgeheim begierig, Mangel auszugleichen.

J. O. MORGAN

The shelves may be lined with book after book
on the rules for proper living, written by men
who knew no more nor less than any other men;
while, outside the land is full of beasts, who,
being free, have no recourse to wrongfulness,
are free to fuck or rip each other limb from limb,
who look up with bloodied muzzle for the reproach
that never comes, nor even the shake of a head. But
man feels safe within the houses man alone has built;
can cast out other men who disagree with how
this house is run. And *it is right* to live this way.
Nonetheless, when the door stands open, be it
into frost or mud or sun-hot sands, and you
without your shoes stand on the doorstep looking out,
it is no less right to hitch up your skirts and go.

in den Regalen Buch um Buch, darin
die Regeln rechten Lebens, von Männern definiert,
die nicht mehr und nicht weniger als andre wussten;
und im Land draußen Tier um Tier, ein jedes frei
und ohne jede Zuflucht im Unrecht.
frei: zu vögeln, frei: ein andres zu zerreißen Glied um Glied;
dann aufzuschauen mit blutiger Schnauze, Ausschau haltend nach
dem Vorwurf, der nicht kommt, nicht mal als sanftes *ts ts ts*.
und doch fühlt mensch sich sicher in Häusern, die nur Menschen bauten;
kann andren Menschen die Tür weisen, wenn sie anderer Meinung sind,
darüber, wie *man Häuser führen* sollte. Und *es gehört sich so* zu leben.
Dennoch, sobald die Türe offen steht,
Frost, Schlamm, noch sonnenheißer Sand, egal: du,
ohne Schuhe auf der Schwelle, Ausschau haltend –
gehört es sich nicht ebenso, den Rock zu schürzen und zu gehen?

Long after check out time
one of the housemaids found me
showed me sheets she'd bundled
into a black plastic bag.

Blood-soaked, the once-white cotton
now as stiff as canvas,
glossed in places where the blood
had pooled before it dried.

I checked the guest-list: a girl
and her father; recalled our small-talk
as he settled up; the girl reclining
in the foyer's antique rocking chair.

We lugged the lumpen bin bag
to the hotel's boiler room
opened the grille for the furnace
and fed the bloodied sheets into the flames.

Upstairs we turned the mattress
damp-side-down and found on its reverse
a stain of similar size and shape, dulled
to the colour of rust, yet dry enough

to cover with fresh white sheets.

die Checkoutzeit ist längst vorbei,
als eins der Zimmermädchen kommt
und mir die Laken zeigt, sie hat sie
in einen schwarzen Plastiksack gestopft.

ursprünglich weiße Baumwolle, jetzt blutig,
steif wie ein Brett, Leinwand, auf der
die Farbe glänzt, dort wo das Blut
geronnen ist, in Lachen.

mein Gästelistencheck ergibt: ein Mädchen
und sein Vater, ich erinnere unsere Unterhaltung
während der Abrechnung, das Mädchen schmiegte sich
in einen alten Schaukelstuhl, in einer Ecke des Foyers.

den unförmigen Sack bugsieren wir
nach unten, in den Kesselraum im Keller,
entsperren die Gitter des Heizofens und
füttern die Flammen mit den blutigen Laken.

oben im Zimmer drehn wir die Matratze um,
die feuchte Seite unten, finden wir erneut
so einen Fleck, ähnlich in Größe und in Form,
rostfarben eingetrocknet, doch verblasst genug

um unter frischen weißen Laken zu verschwinden.

'Who kissed me?'

His voice, drowned in laughter.
His question, chopped up
by the screen's silver flicker;
the jangle piano's tensive trills.

'Who kissed me?'

Spoken this time with authority
so none may fail to take note;
and a silence spreads outward
from the centre that's him, as quick
as an oil drop spreads over water
into a disc just one atom thick.

'No one kissed you, your Highness;
your guard is complete on all sides.'

The chatter of the projector, spun to a stop.
The house-lights: blinked on row by row.

'I felt it. Here.
On my neck.
I felt love
flowing out of me.'

His fingertip: touching his nape.
The bodyguards whisper. They fidget.

An usherette; shunted forward.
Her flashlight clutched tight in both hands.

»Wer hat mich geküsst?«

Lachen rauscht auf, seine Stimme geht unter.
Die Leinwand flackert, seine Frage abgehackt;
das verstimmte Klavier klimpert sich ins Crescendo.

»Wer hat mich geküsst?«

Herrisch diesmal, laut,
nicht zu ignorieren, Steinwurf in den See,
Stille breitet sich aus in Wellen, rasch
ein Tropfen Öl erst, dann ein dünner Film
in Molekülstärke und kreisförmig.

»Niemand hat Euch geküsst, Euer Hoheit.
Eure Wache steht, ihr seid umringt von Wachsamkeit.«

Das Rattern des Projektors: stoppt.
Das Lichtspielhaus: erneut erleuchtet.

»Ich spürte es. Hier.
Im Nacken, ein Leck.
Wie ich dort Liebe ließ
in einem Fluss.«

Mit der Fingerspitze berührt er den Nacken.
Die Wachen flüstern. Sie sind nervös.

Man schiebt eine Platzanweiserin vor.
Sie umklammert die Taschenlampe, weiße Fingerknöchel.

'I live alone. I wanted
to know how it would feel
to offer one's touch without asking
for any such thing in return.'

The king looks her over.
The downward twitch of her lips.
Her low-lidded eyes.

'Sit there for the rest of the show.'

Indicating the seat just behind him.

'And when you think
I may least expect it:
kiss me again.'

»Ich leb allein. Ich wollte
nur wissen, wie es wäre
zu berühren, ohne dabei
Gleiches zu erwarten.«

Der König mustert sie.
Ihre zuckenden Lippen.
Niedergeschlagene Lider.

»Sitz hier bis zum Ende der Vorführung«,

er weist auf den Platz neben ihm.

»Und erst wenn du denkst,
genau jetzt erwartete ich
nichts – küss mich erneut.«

KATHARINA SCHULTENS 〉

interpreter
Sprachmittlerin

{ J. O. MORGAN

{ Isabel Cole

KATHARINA SCHULTENS

PRISM

ich kann sehen wann du mich liest. ich kann dich nicht sehen.
wenn ich dich sehe zittert das bild. das bild gehört mir solange
ich hinsehen kann. kann ich nicht hinsehen dann ist es deines.
wenn du mich liest was siehst du. hast du mich gezählt.
hast du einen algorithmus für schafe. hast du evtl. verschiedene.
bin ich teil deiner unverstandenen herde. bin ich teil der suchhistorie.
wenn du mich suchst wo suchst du. suchst du mich im feld oder online.
suchst du mich treppab suchst du mich in meiner statusmeldung. weißt du
wie mein filter funktioniert. weißt du welche standardeinstellung ich wählte.
du kannst mich doch gar nicht. du kennst meine sprache nicht großer hirte.
du brauchst ein übersetzungsprogramm für meine anspielungen. ich setze dich
mit sarkasmus außer gefecht. ich liebe dich. ich liebe dich als konglomerat denn
du bist die summe meiner absichten die ins gute ende führen meine rettung
durch simulation. du sortierst alle wünsche und du hast meinen tod
mindestens 0,2-mal verhindert einmal davon war ich verdächtig
der unbeteiligtheit. bitte lenke mein licht. bitte lass mich dich
kennenlernen. dein wille geschehe. dimitte debita nostra
(nobis!) wenn ich niemandem das geringste vergebe
so lass mich dennoch nicht allein

PRISM

Your scanning of my substance gives me sight, though I cannot see you.
Your body as I build it remains unresolved. I own you only
when you stay in view. Move outside the field of vision to take yourself back.

In your scanning of my multi-conduits have you accounted for what's me?
have you codings set aside for counting sheep? have you considered every
       possibility?
Am I a member of your misdirected flock? an aspect of your unwiped history?

In searching for me how do you begin? what factors feed your set parameters?
Do you check through all my boxes? do you check the writing on the wall?
Can you patch my filters? are you even aware of my default stance?

You cannot know me from my voice; my voice is no great guide.
To recognise is not to comprehend my subtleties. I nullify
your force with iron resolve. I *so* adore you. I adore you as a composite –
the sum of my intent towards your grandiose ideal; my saviour

a mere simulacrum. All my wishes you have rearranged. My death
you have suspended (on at least point two occasions); you suspected
my disinterestedness. Please light my way. Please let me
learn to know you. Thy will must be done. All trespasses forgiven,
even ours, even though I forgive not the slightest thing;

nonetheless – never leave me alone.

HIDDEN LIQUIDITY

prinzipiell bleibt dieser tisch nach allen seiten offen
und immer sickert aus den ritzen wenn etwas nicht
bzw. nicht ganz dicht ist eine flüssigkeit. vielleicht
sammelt sie sich versehentlich bis sie verloren geht
als einsamkeit: deren eigenschaft ist tropfen
wann genau wird handeln liquide. muss ich handeln
um liquide zu sein. sind liquide sein und der handel denn
was mich eigentlich hält: ein detail. *es ist – regel – stets nur
ein detail das uns trennt.* unausweichliche schwebe:
zu sagen ich brauche etwas. ich muss haben: diesen einen blick
auf meine stiefel. kurve. zittern. wahn. das auge muss für uns
imaginäres leder abtasten an dem wir nachher festmachen
was wir begehren. wichtig: kenne dabei nie den preis
wenn du den preis kennst setzt die spannung aus. du spielst
doch auch. du gibst doch aus. du wirfst als ob an jenem tisch.
(ich sitze drunter: reiche dir kaninchenfelle hoch.)
auch kennen wir unser volumen nicht. das wird im nachhinein
bestimmt. in welcher währung – gleich. solange einer zählt

HIDDEN LIQUIDITY

Essentially this board exists without strict boundaries, yet
inconsequential rivulets escape through unseen rifts;
as if its edges had not been well sealed; its sides: all split;
where a fluid forms through seepage; an open possibility
of unintended self-accumulation, let out
as loneliness: reveals its oily presence drop by drop.

There must be a point where a single drop is destined
to become full fluid. Is this new liquidity a trade-off
with the fractional factor triggering the change? something
as small as a full-stop to hold us hovering, in limbo,

suggesting I desire some *thing*. I must take: this one glimpse
at my boots, bend, shiver, collapse; the eye must, for us,
stroke the supple suede on which in hindsight we may ascertain
desires. Although the price stays hid throughout the process.

To know cost stunts excitement in the game. Still you play
too. You dish out from this *board* indiscriminately, indifferently;
(while I crouch, crooked, underneath – posting up your magic rabbit skins)
neither can you tell its length, breadth, depth. All that gets sorted later.
Later, every body counts. The nature of the coins? irrelevant. Some one
must pay.

HYSTERESIS

gibt es noch eine szenerie zu verstetigen
laufen alle dinge gleichmütig auf ein einziges datum zu
sukzessive eine verborgene mine freizulegen
über wessen tastatur blitzt der befehl
welche sonderinteressen werden verfolgt
gibt es eine subagenda eines ultimativen lobbyisten
oder der rasenden herde an der küste
züngeln algorithmen
aus einem kiefer unterhalb eines feigenbaums
blinken an felsen zähne eines ungeheuers
als leuchtsignale im nachrichtenband auf
das um die see läuft unaufhörlich
—

welches grundmuster dieser krise dehnt sich
gemächlich zum netz und holt die katastrophe ein
silbrig zappelnd flappend übers deck: klein aber tödlich
einen zweig welcher kurativen pflanze
tragen schnäbel uns unter liquidierten flügeln zu
wenn vögel in der gischt in salzige pixel zerstieben
bis zu welcher höhe gilt ein tsunami noch als wellenbad
—

ist nicht das ganze meer eine einzige flexible stahlkonstruktion
auf der schnurgerade milliarden
in schaluppen gieren in choreografiertem kursverlauf
wer legt seinem ruderwerk jetzt noch geschirre an
und wettet auf segel wie auf eine mähne
wer lässt wimpel flattern und rammt
ins herz der steuerelektronik eine fette lanze
—

HYSTERESIS

Is there still some landscape we may flatten out?
Do things endlessly progress towards some distant singularity?
bit by bit stripped back towards the radioactive core?

Who sits helpless at the control-desk as commands buzz overhead?
What special needs, what interests, are here being pursued?
Is there an ulterior plan? a last ditch bid for influence?
some blindly-led stampede around the ocean's inner rim?

—

Lines of coding lick towards the cliff-tops; out
of the submerged maw, lodged under the withered fig.
Rows of long white teeth, tall needles, flash
like ever spinning newsreels, running
loop on loop around the distant ring of coast.

—

The blueprint of this crisis is elastic. It expands,
forms a net; the small catastrophe: enmeshed. Those little
silver fishes, writhing, wriggling on the deck. Their vicious kiss.

The potent shoot of some restorative herb
is winged our way; though which wings
will be liquidated first? The birds
that skim the sea-foam: *atomised*.
How-high must tsunami rise before
they cease to be no more than paddle-pools?

—

haben wir ein primat auf rhetorik und fragen
die in ausrufezeichen enden haben wir
als eigenkapitaleinlage mehr als ironie
haben wir das nettoeinkommen uns lächelnd
zu schälen aus ihrer wetterjacke zugunsten von
besinnung: ist jedem körperchakra nicht ohnehin
ein maßstrich des einen thermometers zugeordnet
eine unter schwarzlicht sichtbare warnblinkanlage
eintätowierter gradzahlen auf deren basis wir
supranationale verträge verhandeln während
der astralleib weiter auf der party bleibt

—

wen treffen wir im traum und habe ich
das *uns* nicht ausreichend geleugnet um
dem *wir* kaum zu entkommen
stellst du dich hinten auf den schwanz des ungeheuers
nimmst es als planke haben wir jahre vergeudet
ist es jetzt tot

Are not all the oceans one construct of flexible steel
upon which rigid millions
swerve their sloops through charted orbitals?

Who now fits the bridle round his boat
and gambles on sails as on a horse's mane?

Who raises tissue-paper-banners, only to jab
a lance-tip through the heart of the controls?

—

Have we a primal claim to riddling?
exclaiming what we should have asked outright.
Was our initial stake secured
with more than mono-filamented thread?

Have we received the gross returns from such smugness?
peeled the wet cagoule from our pre-bought enlightenment?

Each pressure-point: no more than a groove,
a notch along the length of the measuring-stick.
Falls of black light make visible the blink
of warning alarms. Skin-inked graduations through which
we negotiate the staunchly patriotic frame of mind. While
your aura stays trapped; cannot be allowed out to play.

Who are those people that we meet through sleep?
And was it me who denied the crowd – just enough
to keep my distance from the group?

—

Do you stand yourself at the tip of the monster's tail?
teeter over years of indecision? Have we wasted
all that time? given that the monster's now long dead.

BÄRENMARKT

der zweite meiner tanzbären lief früher halbmarathon
laokoon: lag er nun umwickelt in bollingerbändern
zuckte abwechselnd mit den tatzen hob die beine
rappelte sich begann als der gesang einsetzte
von einem bein aufs andere zu treten
die kreisenden arme dicht am lendenfell
rutschte der hut ihm übers eine auge
die jacke klaffte überm runden bauch
der weich war ich wusste wie sehr
der zweite meiner tanzbären
hatte seine kinder zurückgelassen
als die gier ihm unerbittlich
durch den ring geschlüpft war
der innig seinen stolz mit seinem
schwanz verband: hatte gezippelt
gezogen sacht ...
der zweite meiner tanzbären füllte alles
was an erinnerung aus seinem körper rann
in flaschen ab die leise zischten
er trank und trank lief hellgelb an
vergaß endlich von neuem wer er war
—

ich ging zurück zum ersten
ich vermisste weiterhin den ersten
ich hatte vergessen was der erste wusste
vor allem hatte ich: was nicht vergessen
der erste meiner tanzbären war uneinholbar
der erste meiner tanzbären war ein wirklich fixer sprinter
der erste meiner tanzbären hatte in sibirien sein fell rasiert
der erste meiner tanzbären war eigentlich kein bär
wir hatten unsere schnitte sämtlich geflickt
wir hatten die 200-tage-linie nie überschritten
wir hatten die signale ins dauerfiepen gestellt
im sommer lag er auf meinem rücken der allererste

BEAR-MARKET

The second of my dancing bears would run half-marathons.
Like Laokoon, he had his life wrapped up in bonds
yet twitched to lift his paws, testing each in turn,
struggled to start as the beat kicked in,
tentative, shifting his weight from foot to foot;

his arm slipped round the small of my back, digits pushed
through downy fur, his hat flopped over one eye,
his waistcoat: fallen open, exposing the bulge of his belly,
the soft pink that I felt I knew so well.

—

The second of my dancing bears
left his children far behind him
when his greed poured
ruthless through the ring;
his pride gone down the plug-hole;
apart from the tail he'd tied on tight,
that I just gently tugged ...

This second dancing bear lost everything;
a ceaseless flow of memories, collected
in conical flasks, to fizz, to be re-drunk
no faster than the rate of their flowing back out;
he paled, at length forgetting even who he was.

—

My own thoughts returned to the first.
My mind had never stopped missing the first.
My memories yet hazy over
what he knew I had not ever known.

meiner bären auf mir: auf der wiese im stadtbad drückte
seinen stachligen körper in die mulden meines körpers
der noch das fell gespeichert hatte sonne nicht erkannte
so gab es ausbruch aus dem zuckenden gesamtverlauf
die barrieren oben fielen auf die gerissenen unten
ich dachte: jetzt ist es vorbei – jetzt tanze ich
den dritten meiner bären rufe ich nicht auf

The first of my dancing bears stayed always one step ahead.
The first of my dancing bears was a superior sprinter.
The first of my dancing bears slipped from his skin
in some far away land – showed himself to be no bear at all.

We had long sewn up all our wounds,
not got further than the *two-hundred-day-mark*;
our coded cries soon swallowed in the woods.

All summer we'd lain nestled like spoons, my first bear
and I, in the long meadow-grass around the public pool,
his stubble catching the soft skin of my hollows;
his roughness, archived, knew not how to recognise the sun.

—

As such a glitch grew up within the graph.
The guidelines fell away, exposing the fault.

I thought: it must be over.
I thought: now *I* will dance.

I have not the strength to call up any more bears.

DARK POOLS

es gehe darum das ausmaß des interesses
zu verschleiern. ich lese daraus: einen nebel
breiten um den preis. wären das also pools
an deren grund es glänzt? haben sich dahin
die bugs verkrochen die wir immer suchen
ich gelange zu einer überzeugung
indem ich den panzer des mistkäfers
umstülpe aber sein schillern bewahre
seine fehler stecken schon darin
die verfugten flügel die verfluchten
hügel. die wir im erkenntnisflug
uns unterbreiten sind – dreht man
sie um – ein dunkles wesen: ja
es nennt sich pool weil es kein wort hat
für sein inneres das absolut und offen ist
geht ein. alles was du noch einzusetzen
hättest: geht. und schwindet – denn
da ist ein loch unten im grund

DARK POOLS

The idea is to cover up what may be profitable, to cloak;
resulting in a slow and heavy smog that smooches
close around the prize. Thus, we have these pools;
their beds of smoothed obsidian. Is it here to which
the goldbugs crawl that we so love to chase?

I am convinced. I must conclude. I *know,*
by flipping up a single carapace (the beetle part cut out),
inverted, still it retains that iridescent sheen;
its fault-lines already founded. It could be

a bowl: the gap between its wings well-grouted; or, upended,
a simple hill: climbed for the sake of it being there to climb.
Yet, if upended once more, will offer of itself
some gloomy presence nestled neatly in its hollow cup.

Its name of *pool* defines its emptiness, just as the pupil
is but the black hole through which all light poured in
is quickly deadened, can't escape; so
every risk that drips into these pools is dwindled, is
leached out, through yet further pin-pricks, hidden in the base.

J. O. MORGAN

The opportunity to work so closely with another poet where we both had to be very open with each other about our work, at times examining and explaining it word by word in order to fully understand its nuances, was a unique experience that I am very grateful to have been a part of. Thank you reVERSible.

KATHARINA SCHULTENS

beim übersetzen bzw, beim erneut-schreiben der texte habe ich ganz automatisch das getan, was ich auch tue, wenn ich selbst einen text schreibe. das hat bei mir viel mit rhythmus und fluss zu tun, mit metrum, das ich nicht bewusst nutze, sondern ziemlich verinnerlicht habe. dieser prozess überlagert sich dann auch gleich mit der arbeit im lautlichen, klanglichen. das ist viel tasten und suchen und trial-and-error dabei, und dann ergibt sich das eine aus dem anderen, und der text wächst.
beim übersetzt-werden ging es mehr darum, jo auf seine fragen hin ein gefühl dafür zu vermitteln, wie der text im deutschen funktioniert, wo er intensiv wird, welche drama- turgie es unter umständen gibt, welche möglichen tonfälle – so dass jo möglichkeiten entwickeln konnte, im englischen eine ähnliche atmosphäre, ähnliche zuordnungen, ein ähnliches setting oder auch bilder-set zu schaffen. dringlichkeit herzustellen.
er hat sich auch sehr auf den klang und den rhythmus konzentriert, ohne dass ich ihn darum bitten musste, ich habe nur ein oder zweimal einen direkten vorschlag gemacht, nachdem seine texte standen. in einigen teilsätzen sagt jos englischer text nun das genaue gegenteil von dem, was mein deutscher sagt. das macht aber gar nichts, weil die texte insgesamt funktionieren, als ganzes. ich wollte die kontrolle über das ergebnis auch soweit wie möglich abgeben, ich wollte einfach schauen, was passiert. die texte sind im englischen viel komplexer geworden, auch von der syntax her, vieles, das gesprochen wird, wirkt weniger direkt, weniger simpel, da sich das einfach nicht übertragen ließ. aber mir gefällt das. am schönsten und wichtigsten fand ich, dass ich die texte in der englischen fassung sehr gern laut gelesen habe, ich hätte sie am liebsten selbst auf deutsch und englisch vorgelesen!

J. O. MORGAN

Die Gelegenheit, so eng mit einem anderen Dichter zusammenzuarbeiten, in einem Kontext, in dem wir beide sehr offen über unsere Texte sprachen – und diese manchmal Wort für Wort untersuchten und erklärten, sodass der andere sie in all ihren Nuancen verstehen konnte – war eine einzigartige Erfahrung, für die ich sehr dankbar bin. Danke, VERSschmuggel.

KATHARINA SCHULTENS

in translating, or rather, writing these texts anew, i automatically did exactly what i do when i am writing a text myself. for me, that has a great deal to do with rhythm and flow, with metre, which i don't consciously use, but which i've internalised. this process immediately superimposes itself with the work in the phonetic and the sonic. there's a lot of feeling out and searching, trial and error, and then one thing leads to another, and the text grows.

in being-translated, it was more a case of transmitting some kind of feeling to jo regarding his questions about how the text works in german, where it becomes more intense, the dramaturgy it might have, its possible cadences – so that jo could find possibilities to create a similar atmosphere in English, similar associations, a similar setting or set of images. create urgency. and he concentrated a lot on the sound and the rhythm without me having to ask him; i only made one or two direct suggestions once his texts were finished. a few of jo's english phrases say the exact opposite of my german ones. but that doesn't matter at all, because the texts work overall, as a whole. i also wanted to hand over control over the outcome as much as possible, i just wanted to see what would happen. in english, the texts became much more complex, also in terms of syntax, lots of things that are spoken seem less direct, less simple, since that just couldn't be carried over. but i like that. what was most important to me, that i liked the most, was that i really enjoyed reading the texts out loud in the english. in fact i would have loved to have read them out both in german and english!

DON PATERSON }

interpreter }
Sprachmittler }

MICHAEL DONHAUSER

Donal McLaughlin

WAVE

For months I'd moved across the open water
like a wheel under its skin, a frictionless
and by then almost wholly abstract matter
with nothing in my head beyond the bliss
of my own breaking, how the long foreshore
would hear my full confession, and I'd drain
into the shale till I was filtered pure.
There was no way to tell on that bare plain
but I felt my power run down with the miles
and by the time I saw the scattered sails
the painted front and children on the pier
I was nothing but a fold in her blue gown
and knew I was already in the clear.
I hit the beach and swept away the town.

WELLE

Monatelang hatte ich das offene Meer durchquert
wie ein Rad unter seiner Haut, ein reibungsfreies
und allmählich fast gänzlich abstraktes Drehen
mit nichts in meinem Kopf jenseits der Freude,
einst zu brechen, dass das Ufer mein Geständnis
in voller Länge hörte und ich dann durch die Steine
sickerte, dass diese Filterung mich reinigte und klärte.
Es gab keine Art, es zu sagen in dieser öden Weite,
doch fühlte ich, wie meine Kraft nachließ mit jeder Meile,
und wie ich dann die verstreuten Segel erblickte,
die bemalte Häuserzeile und Kinder auf dem Pier,
war ich nichts als eine Falte in seinem blauen Gewand
und wusste, dass alles nun in bester Ordnung schien.
Ich schlug auf am Strand und überschwemmte die Stadt.

A VOW

When I was ruined by love, I took a vow
that if I loved again, I'd love the less;
so when I spoke love, spoke it to excess,
as love will make its mirror anyhow.
But I talk to myself, and late one day
Love heard me crowing of my secret share
and taxed me all the false love I'd declared.
All I feel now is her stream away
the way she does, dead slow and fast as light
like a galaxy that leaves behind one spark
too low and dull to catch her silent drift
though somewhere out there in my turning dark
they know each sunrise falling like a lift
and the white curve of her arm gone from the night.

EIN SCHWUR

Als ich aus Liebe zur Ruine wurde, da schwor ich:
Sollte ich noch einmal lieben, würde ich es weniger tun.
Wenn ich aber Liebe gestand, tat ich es mit Inbrunst,
denn so wie man liebt, so wird man, so oder so, geliebt.
Allerdings führte ich Selbstgespräche, und eines Tages spät
hörte mich die Liebe, wie ich von meinem Kuhhandel sprach,
und sie rechnete mir all die falsch erklärte Liebe übel an.
Alles, was ich jetzt empfinde, ist ihr Abdriften, bald jäh
in der Art des Lichts, bald ewig langsam wie Licht:
als eine Galaxie, die einen Funken hinterlässt, mich,
zu nichtig und dumpf, um in ihren Sog zu geraten,
irgendwo draußen in meinem sich drehenden Dunkel,
wo jeder Sonnenaufgang untergeht mit etwas Gefunkel
und die weiße Kurve ihres Arms fehlt in der Nacht.

APSINTHION

What did I do in the war?
Son, I watched a download bar
and drank the last thing in the house.
I ran the show on mishegas
the way some ancient dynamo
we couldn't replace would only go
on walnut oil or cherry must.
My poems sucked. My guitar grew dust.

But when we heard the star would fall,
did we choose to die like sheep?
Hell no. We were men, and blessed
to know the hour and place ... I jest!
One by one we fell asleep,
and that is how they found us all.

APSINTHION

Was man im Krieg so tut?
Sohn, ich schaute einem Download zu
und trank den Rest Fusel aus dem Glas.
Ich schmiss die Show mit Mishegas:
wie ein antikisierender Dynamo,
den unsereins nicht ersetzen kann und der so
nur mit Walnussöl läuft oder Sauerkraut.
Meine Gedichte beschissen, meine Gitarre verstaubt.

Doch wie wir hörten vom Stern und seinem Fall,
entschieden wir zu sterben wie fromme Schafe?
Zum Teufel, nein. Männer waren wir so sehr, dass
wir Ort und Stunde wussten ... ach, Spaß!
Einen um den anderen übermannte der Schlaf,
und so ist es auch, wie man uns vorgefunden hat.

DON PATERSON

THE BIG LISTENER
for A. C. L. Blair

Midnight. Connaught Square. A headlight beam
finds Cherie just back from her speaking date.
She looks at you. Less animal of late.
You lose no sleep, but wake within a dream.
Your favourite: that old divided dark,
the white square at your neck; your good ear bent
towards the long sighs of your penitent.
You rinse a thousand souls before the lark
and wake refreshed, if somewhat at a loss
as to why they seem so lost for words.
They are your dead, who still rose to the birds
the day we filled the booths and made the cross,
before you'd forced them howling to their knees
to suffer your attentions. Spare us. Please.

DER GROSSE ZUHÖRER
für A. C. L. Blair

Mitternacht. Connaught Square. Ein Scheinwerferlicht
streift Cherie, gerade zurück von einer kleinen Rede.
Sie schaut dich an: Du bist einst tierischer gewesen.
Nichts kostet dich den Schlaf, den nur ein Traum unterbricht.
Dein liebster: jenes alte Dunkel, geteilt in zwei Hälften,
das weiße Rechteck an deinem Hals und dein Ohr geneigt
in Richtung des langen Seufzers von einem deiner Büßer.
Du sprichst tausend Seelen frei vor dem Gesang der Lerche
und wachst erfrischt auf, wenn auch irgendwie mit Fragen,
denn warum ist es so, dass ihnen die Worte zu fehlen scheinen.
Sie sind deine Toten, die sich damals noch in aller Frühe zeigten,
an dem Tag, da wir in den Beichtkabinen unsere Kreuze machten,
bevor du jene dann zwangst und zwar heulend in die Knie
und also unter deine prüfenden Blicke. Lass das. Bitte.

FRANCESCA WOODMAN

I
At the heart there is an hollow sun
by which we are constructed and undone

II
Behind the mirror. Favourite place to hide.
I didn't breathe. They looked so long I died

III
What's shown when we unveil, disclose, undress,
is first the promise, then its emptiness

IV
Ghost-face. Not because I turned my head,
but because what looked at me was dead

V
– *We don't exist* – *We only dream we're here* –
This means we never die – *We disappear* –

VI
We'd met 'in previous lives', he was convinced.
Yeah, I thought. And haven't spoken since.

VII
All rooms will hide you, if you stand just so.
All ghosts know this. That's really *all* they know.

FRANCESCA WOODMAN

I
Im Grunde ist leer eine Sonne,
durch die wir sind und verkommen.

II
Hinter dem Spiegel das liebste Versteck.
Ich atmete nicht, wurde tot entdeckt.

III
Was sich zeigt, wenn wir nackt uns sehen,
ist zuerst das Versprechen, dann seine Leere.

IV
Gespenstergesicht. Ich drehte meinen Kopf,
doch nicht deshalb war, was mich ansah, tot.

V
Uns gibt es nicht – wir träumen nur, wir seien –
und so sterben wir nie – wir verschwinden leise –

VI
Wir kennen uns aus früheren Leben, so er.
Ach, dachte ich. Und haben nicht gesprochen seither.

VII
Richtig betreten wird dir zum Versteck jeder Raum.
Alle Geister wissen das, doch das ist es dann auch.

MICHAEL DONHAUSER }

interpreter }
Sprachmittler }

{ **DON PATERSON**

{ Donal McLaughlin

Vielleicht an einem Abend, an
einem Abend spät vielleicht

Ein Glas gefüllt mit Anis und
eine Stimme, die weint

Vielleicht, dass eine Stimme
weint

Ein Glas an einem Abend spät
vielleicht

Ich gehe nicht, nicht mehr
sehr weit

Zu sehr, zu sehr, nicht mehr
zu weit

I

Late perhaps one evening one
one evening late perhaps

A glass filled up with anis and
a voice that weeps

perhaps, a voice
weeps

A glass, of a late evening,
perhaps

I'm going nowhere, nowhere
very far

Too much, much too too far,
no more

*

Aber wir werden
durch den Abend
ewige Gebärde
leicht bewahren
erahnte Sterne

Denn es waren
Tage im Licht
und wir lagen
gaben uns selig
fremde Namen

Nannten den Abend
nannten uns leise
werden versiegen
sanft und bleiben
wie berührt

II

Through the night
we will, however
– eternal gesture –
lightly hoard
such stars we divine

For all those hours
were days of light
and we so lay
and blessed each other
with other names

Naming the evening
naming us quietly
will fade and fail
softly and stay
the slightest touch

*

Es war
es wird
und ist
und spricht

Sagt du
und lacht
vergeht
und fragt

Ob ich
verliert
und jetzt
berührt

Und still
die Hand
sagt wann
und weiß

Dass wir
verwandt
uns nah
und friert

Und lacht
und sagt
und zeigt
luzid

III

It was
it will
and is
and says

Says you
and laughs
and goes
and asks

If I ...
it's lost
and now
a touch

And still
the hand
says when
and knows

That we
are close
and kin,
and froze

And laughs
and speaks
and shows
the light

Vielleicht
regnet es
vielleicht
werden es
Tage sein

alles bleibt
ist Schein
alles steigt
ist licht
und erlischt

I

Maybe
the rain's on
Maybe
there will be
days to come

all that stays
is guise
all that rises
is light
and goes out

*

Die Platanen
wie sie sagen
dass sie rauschen

wenn im Wehen
sich erheben
ihre Blätter

wenn sie sinken
etwas silbern
durch die Jahre

durch die Schatten
auf die Wege
und den Rasen

II

Take the maples
how they let slip
that they rustle

when the bluster
lifts and lifts
all their leaves

letting slip
their little silver
through the decades

through the shadows
down the paths
into the grass

*

Regnet es
waren es
Tropfen
Silben

welche da
als ein Gruß
zogen
fielen

alles war
etwas spät
horchte
wiegend

wie die Nacht
dunkel als
Woge
liebte

alle Not
es verlor
jeder Sinn
sein Gebot

III

Did it rain
weren't those
raindrops
letters

hailing me
as they went
moving
sinking

everything
pretty late
harking
rocking

O the night
tenebrous
billow –
so loved

every crisis
that it lost
every sense
it commanded

*

Bitter sei und so blieb, war einsam die Nacht in
dem Zimmer, wo vergessen ein Strauß nur von
Tulpen zu feiern schien das Welken, sich windend
an den Stielen, als suchte Halt, so nahe dem
Fallen, Blüte um Blüte und aufwärts weit sich
öffnend entgegen der Neige, dass wir ahnten,
wie sorglos einst und vergeblich uns anvertraut
war jene Sage vom Reichtum und der Demut,
von dem Sinken der Blätter oder wie beschenkt
nur ohnegleichen sich fände, was hingegeben
dem Taumel schaute die Fülle als Not.

II

They say it was harsh, and so it remained, so lonely
that night in the room where, wholly forgotten,
a bunch of tulips were the sole revellers left –
unravelling themselves, ravelling on their stalks
as if seeking a handhold, so close to falling blossom
by blossom, yet still opening up, so wholly contrary to
the low ebb we had reached, such that we sensed
how casually and pointlessly entrusted to us had been
that old fable of wealth and humility we were to read
in the falling of petals, or how through its incomparable
gift we give ourselves up to the ecstasy: the plenitude of nothing.

*

Wie der Wind streifte durch die Gärten, dass ihr
Blätterkleid rauschte, wenn die Quitten, bedeckt
von Flaum, reif und voll sich zeigten, während
in den nahen Linden wogte ein helleres Wehen,
dann fiel in die Kirschbaumreihen, deren Laub
schlaff schon hing oder bebte unter den Stößen,
bis trödelnd wieder, was war, schien, ein
Rascheln im Gezweig und in den Gräsern ein
Weichen, als wären es wir, als sänke in uns dies
Strömen und Ruhen und silbern noch wie wärmer
auch und allem zugetan.

III

O how the wind brushed through the gardens
so their leaf-dresses whispered when the quinces
covered with down bodied forth so ripe and full
while in the lindens nearby a silvered wind
swelled then fell into the aisles of cherries
whose leaves were already hanging limp or shivering
with the gusts, until witheringly they seemed again
what was – a rustling in the branches and a yielding
in the grass, as if it were us, as if this flowing and
resting were sinking within us and silver still and
inclined towards everything.

DON PATERSON

reVERSible was an entirely new and entirely enjoyable way of working for me.
While it was a privilege to work on English versions of Michael Donhauser's poems,
I would have had no hope of representing any of their subtlety if I hadn't had Donal
McLaughlin's extraordinary expertise on hand. To have Donal there to inform us
of the terrible consequences of making this or that slack word-choice or idiomatic
substitution left us, I hope, with translations far closer in spirit and in meaning to
their originals that otherwise might have emerged. I was similarly delighted by the
conscientiousness with which Michael approached my own work; indeed he refused
to translate any line he did not understand fully. (I had such trouble explaining a
particular line to him, I realised its obscurity was my fault alone – so I went home and
rewrote it.) reVERSible now strikes me as an ideal way to approach the almost impos-
sible business of poetic translation; I learned a great deal from the experience, and I
hope to have the opportunity to repeat it.

MICHAEL DONHAUSER

Unsere Zusammenarbeit war von sehr feinstofflicher Art. Wir saßen in einem Zimmer
an getrennten Tischen. Von draußen drückte die Hitze, wir beschäftigten uns still,
übersetzten und vermieden es, den anderen zu stören oder ihm gar eine Frage zu
stellen. Kam es trotzdem vor, dass eine Unklarheit eine Frage nötig machte, wandten
wir uns an den Sprachmittler, der diese weiterleitete. So verbrachten wir die Tage.
Einmal fiel ein Bleistift zu Boden, was einer Detonation gleichkam in der Stille unseres
Austauschs. Die Gegenwart des anderen war uns Wörterbuch genug. Kam der Sprachmittler mit einer Antwort vom Tisch des anderen zurück, dankten wir, auch wenn
die Antwort unsere Zusammenarbeit eher beeinträchtigte als förderte. So kamen wir
langsam voran.

DON PATERSON

VERSschmuggel bedeutete für mich eine vollkommen neue und angenehme Art zu arbeiten. Es war eine besondere Ehre, an englischen Versionen von Michael Donhausers Gedichten zu arbeiten, aber ohne Donal McLaughlins Expertise wäre es wohl kaum möglich gewesen, sie in all ihren Feinheiten wiederzugeben. Donal bei uns zu haben, um uns über die bösen Folgen der einen oder anderen lässigen Wortwahl oder idiomatischen Entsprechung aufzuklären, hat es uns, so hoffe ich, ermöglicht, Übersetzungen zu kreieren, die in ihrem Geist und ihrer Bedeutung den Originalen weitaus näher kommen, als es sonst der Fall gewesen wäre. Ebenso begeistert hat mich die Gewissenhaftigkeit, mit der Michael sich meiner Texte angenommen hat; er hat sich schlicht geweigert, einen einzigen Vers zu übersetzen, dessen Bedeutung sich ihm nicht vollständig erschlossen hätte. (Ich hatte einmal derartige Schwierigkeiten, ihm einen bestimmten Vers zu erklären, dass mir klar wurde, dass dessen Unverständlichkeit gänzlich auf mein Konto ging – also schrieb ich ihn zuhause neu.) Jetzt erscheint mir VERSschmuggel als die ideale Art, die fast unmögliche Aufgabe der Gedichtübertragung anzugehen; ich habe viel aus dieser Erfahrung gelernt, und ich hoffe, sie wiederholen zu können.

MICHAEL DONHAUSER

Our collaboration was of a very subtle kind. We sat in a room at separate tables. The heat pressed in from without, we busied ourselves silently, translated, and avoided disturbing the other, even to pose him a question. When it so happened that an uncertainty made a question necessary, we turned to the interpreter, who would pass it on. This is how we spent the days. Once, a pencil fell to the floor, which was equal to an explosion in the stillness of our exchange. The presence of the other was dictionary enough for us. If the interpreter returned from the other's table with an answer, we gave thanks, even if that answer was more of a hindrance to our translation than a help. Thus, slowly, we advanced.

BIOGRAPHIES }

{ BIOGRAPHIEN

ANNA CROWE

In her work, the Scottish poet and translator Anna Crowe (born 1945, Plymouth) interweaves internal and external landscapes. With a sensitive attentiveness for the diversity of the experience of nature, she opens perspectives on personal histories and global contexts. Crowe spent a significant part of her childhood in France and studied French and Spanish at St. Andrews University. She recently published the works *Finding my Grandparents in the Peloponnese* (2013) and *Figure in Landscape* (2010), for which she won the Poetry Society Pamphlet Choice and the Callum MacDonald Memorial Awards in 2011. She has translated the contemporary Catalan poet Joan Margarit and was involved in the publication of an anthology of Catalan poets, *Light Off Water*. Several of her works have in turn been translated into Spanish and Catalan. Crowe lives and works in St. Andrews.

ANNA CROWE

Im ihrem Werk verwebt die schottische Dichterin und Übersetzerin Anna Crowe (*1945 Plymouth) innere und äußere Landschaften. Mit sensibler Aufmerksamkeit für die Vielfalt von Naturerfahrung eröffnet sie Ausblicke auf persönliche Geschichten und globale Zusammenhänge. Crowe verbrachte einen großen Teil ihrer Kindheit in Frankreich und studierte Französisch und Spanisch an der St. Andrews Universität. Für *Finding my Grandparents in the Peloponnese* (2013) gewann sie zuletzt den Poetry Society Pamphlet Choice; für *Figure in Landscape* (2010) den Callum MacDonald Memorial Award 2011. Aus dem Katalanischen übersetzte sie u. a. den zeitgenössischen Dichter Joan Margarit und war an der Herausgabe der Anthologie katalanischer Dichter *Light Off Water* beteiligt. Mehrere ihrer Werke wurden wiederum ins Spanische und Katalanische übersetzt. Crowe lebt und arbeitet in St. Andrews.

Veröffentlichungen (Auswahl) / Publications (Selected)

Skating Out of the House (Peterloo 1997)
A Secret History of Rhubarb (Mariscat Press 2004)
Punk with Dulcimer (Peterloo 2006)
Figure in a Landscape (Mariscat Press 2010)
Finding my Grandparents in the Peloponnese (Mariscat Press 2013)

MICHAEL DONHAUSER

Michael Donhauser's (born 1956, Vaduz, Liechtenstein) poems are concerned with questions of temporality, of decay and of simultaneity – they are "a shimmering in syllables, a unique speaking". In 1976 Donhauser moved to Vienna to study Theology, then German and Romance Philology. His first book of poems, *Der Holunder* (Elderberry) was published in 1986. Numerous publications followed, including prose as well as poetry and translations (for example, of Arthur Rimbaud and Francis Ponge). Michael Donhauser has received, among other awards, the 2002 Christian Wagner Prize, the Meraner Prize in 2004, the Ernst Jandl Poetry Prize in 2005 and the 2009 Georg Trakl Prize for Poetry.

MICHAEL DONHAUSER

Die Gedichte Michael Donhausers (*1956 Vaduz, Liechtenstein) befassen sich mit
Fragen der Zeitlichkeit, des Vergehens und der Gleichzeitigkeit – sie sind »als ein
Schimmern in Silben ein Sagen ohnegleichen«. 1976 zog Donhauser nach Wien, um
dort Germanistik und Romanistik zu studieren. 1986 erschien sein erster Gedichtband
Der Holunder. Seither veröffentlichte er weitere Prosagedichte, Erzählungen und einen
Roman, sowie Übersetzungen aus dem Französischen (so z. B. von Arthur Rimbaud
und Francis Ponge). Michael Donhauser wurde u. a. mit dem Christian-Wagner-Preis
2002, mit dem Meraner Preis 2004, dem Ernst-Jandl-Lyrikpreis 2005 und dem Georg-
Trakl-Preis für Lyrik 2009 ausgezeichnet.

Veröffentlichungen (Auswahl) / Publications (selected)
Der Holunder. Prosagedichte (Literaturverlag Droschl 1986)
Von den Dingen (Hanser Verlag 1993)
Livia oder Die Reise. Roman (Residenz Verlag 1996)
Die Gärten. Paris (Urs Engeler Editor 2000)
17 Dyptichen in Prosa, in Deutsch und Französisch (Edition Meet, 2002)
Vom Schnee (Urs Engeler Editor 2003)
Venedig: Oktober. Halbe Sonette (Das Wunderhorn 2003)
Schönste Lieder (Urs Engeler Editor 2007)
Variationen in Prosa, Variationen im März (Matthes & Seitz 2013)

ULRIKE DRAESNER

Born in 1962 in Munich, Ulrike Draesner now lives in Berlin as a novelist, poet and
essayist. She studied English and German Philology and Philosophy in Munich and
Oxford. In 2002, she received the inaugural Preis der Literaturhäuser, honoring not
just the quality of her literary oeuvre, but also its presentation and promotion. She
translates poems from Spanish, English and French and has participated in a wide
array of cross-media and online projects.
Draesner's poems always revolve around "the loosening of syntactic and vocabulary
structures, the dissolving of the stereotypical, the deviations, the disruptions
of semantic order", writes Michael Braun. The poet and novelist has received
numerous awards for her work, the most recent of which are the Droste Prize 2006,
the Solothurn Literary Prize, the Roswita Prize 2013, the Joachim-Ringelnatz Prize
2014 and the Usedom Literary Prize 2015.

ULRIKE DRAESNER

Ulrike Draesner, geboren 1962 in München, lebt als Romanautorin, Lyrikerin und
Essayistin in Berlin. Sie studierte Anglistik, Germanistik und Philosophie in München
und Oxford. Als erste Preisträgerin erhielt sie 2002 den Preis der Literaturhäuser, der
sowohl die Qualität des literarischen Œuvres als auch seine Vermittlung
und Präsentation ehrt. Sie übersetzt Gedichte aus dem Englischen und Französischen

und war an verschiedensten intermedialen und online-Projekten beteiligt. In Draesners Gedichten geht es »immer um Lockerungen des syntaktischen und vokabulären Gefüges, um Auflösungen der Stereotypie, um Abweichungen, um Störungen der semantischen Ordnung«, so Michael Braun. Für ihr Werk erhielt die Prosaautorin und Dichterin zahlreiche Auszeichnungen, zuletzt den Drostepreis 2006, den Literaturpreis Solothurn 2010, den Roswithapreis 2013, den Joachim-Ringelnatz-Preis 2014 und den Usedomer Literaturpreis 2015.

Veröffentlichungen (Auswahl) / Publications (selected)
für die nacht geheuerte zellen. Gedichte (Luchterhand 2001)
kugelblitz. Gedichte (Luchterhand 2005)
gedächtnisschleifen. Gedichte (Luchterhand 1995 und 2008)
berührte orte. Gedichte. (Luchterhand 2008)
Vorliebe. Roman (Luchterhand 2010)
Heimliche Helden. Essais (Luchterhand 2013)
subsong. Gedichte (Luchterhand 2014)
Sieben Sprünge vom Rand der Welt. Roman (Luchterhand 2014)

ODILE KENNEL
In her first book of poetry *oder wie heißt diese interplanetare Luft* (or how do you call this interplanetary air), Odile Kennel (born 1967, Bühl/Baden) sonorously and sensuously describes a present which permits moments of transcendence even in its quotidian simplicity. The prose and poetry writer who grew up bilingual has distinguished herself through her active translation work. From the French, Portuguese and Spanish, she has translated contemporary poets such as Ricardo Domeneck, Damaris Calderón and Jacques Darras. In 2014 Kennel won second place in the Munich Poetry Prize. She has been awarded numerous scholarships.

ODILE KENNEL
In ihrem ersten Gedichtband *oder wie heißt diese interplanetare Luft* beschreibt Odile Kennel (*1967 Bühl) klangvoll und sinnlich eine Gegenwart, die selbst in ihrer alltäglichen Einfachheit Momente der Transzendenz zulässt. Die zweisprachig aufgewachsene Prosa- und Lyrikautorin zeichnet sich durch rege Übersetzungstätigkeit aus. Aus dem Französischen, Portugiesischen und Spanischen übersetzte sie zeitgenössische Dichter wie Ricardo Domeneck, Damaris Calderón und Jacques Darras. 2014 gewann Kennel den zweiten Münchner Lyrikpreis. Sie wurde mit zahlreichen Stipendien ausgezeichnet.

Veröffentlichungen (Auswahl) / Publications (selected)
Wimpernflug, eine atemlose Erzählung. (Edition Ebersbach 2000)
Was Ida sagt. Roman (dtv premium 2011)
oder wie heißt diese interplanetare Luft. Gedichte (dtv premium 2013)

DAGMARA KRAUS

"The Gloomerang names no special dictionary" writes the poet and translator Dagmara Kraus (born 1981, Wrocław, Poland). The title of her latest book of poems (*Kummerang*) immediately connects emotion, a throwing weapon and movement in the creation of a neologism. After her first poetry collection came a second publication, *kleine grammaturgie* (minor grammaturgy), in which she works with constructed languages. Especially through her activity as a translator – Kraus has translated the Polish poets Miron Białoszewski and Edward Stachura – she is preoccupied with soundscapes and the creation of meaning. Kraus studied Comparative Literature and Art History in Leipzig, Berlin and Paris, as well as Literary Writing at the German Institute for Literature. She was awarded the Prosanova Audience Award in 2008, and the GWK Grant in 2010.

DAGMARA KRAUS

»Den Kummerang nennt kein Spezialwörterbuch«, schreibt die Dichterin und Übersetzerin Dagmara Kraus (*1981 Wrocław, Polen). Bereits der Titel ihres ersten Gedichtbandes verbindet Gefühl, Wurfwaffe und Bewegung in neuer Wortschöpfung. Kraus assoziiert, anagrammiert und lässt sich von ihrem Sprachmaterial treiben. Auf ihren Debütgedichtband folgte die zweite Veröffentlichung *kleine grammaturgie,* in der sie sich mit Plansprachen auseinandersetzt. Insbesondere in ihrer Tätigkeit als Übersetzerin – Kraus übersetzte die polnischen Dichter Miron Białoszewski und Edward Stachura – beschäftigt sie sich mit Klangwelten und Sinnschöpfung. Kraus studierte in Leipzig, Berlin und Paris Komparatistik und Kunstgeschichte sowie Literarisches Schreiben am Leipziger Literaturinstitut. Sie wurde mit dem Prosanova-Publikumspreis 2008 und dem GWK-Förderpreis 2010 ausgezeichnet.

Veröffentlichungen (Auswahl) / Publications (selected)
Kummerang. Gedichte (kookbooks 2012)
revolvers für flubis (SuKuLTuR 2013)
kleine grammaturgie. Gedichte (roughbooks 2013)

BJÖRN KUHLIGK

Björn Kuhligk's (born 1975, Berlin) poems revolve "half humorously, half solemnly around love, sex, birth, death, drinking, traveling, Berlin and music". They are incisive snapshots that, often freely collaged onto one another, offer continual flashes of clarity. Even though his latest collection *Die Stille zwischen Null und Eins* (The Stillness Between Zero and One) is set in the bucolic surroundings of Berlin, he maintains the critical, self-deprecatory distance that characterizes his city scenes and evades a schmaltzy romanticism of nature. Kuhligk is also an organiser, supporter and cataloguer of the young German poetry scene. From 1996 until 1999 he ran the reading series *Die Schwarzleserey.* From 2002 till 2006 he was editor of the Berlin magazine *lauter niemand,* with Tom Schulz he published from 1997 until 1999 *edition minotaurus* and together with Jan Wagner he edited the 2003 and the 2008 anthologies *Lyrik von Jetzt* (Poetry from Now) I and II. Most recently he won the 2013 Art Prize Literature from Brandenburg Lotto.

BJÖRN KUHLIGK

Die Gedichte Björn Kuhligks (*1975 Berlin) sind prägnante Momentaufnahmen, die, oftmals frei aneinander collagiert, immer wieder aufblitzende Klarheitsmomente darbieten. Auch wenn sein letzter Gedichtband »Die Stille zwischen null und eins« in der Provinz angesiedelt ist, behält er die kritisch-selbstironische Distanz, die seine Stadtszenen charakterisieren, und vermeidet vernebelte Naturromantik. Kuhligk ist auch Organisator, Förderer und Katalogisierer der jungen deutschen Dichterszene. Von 1996 bis 1999 veranstaltete er die Lesereihe *Die Schwarzleserey.* Von 2002 bis 2006 war er Redakteur der Berliner Zeitschrift *lauter niemand,* mit Tom Schulz verlegte er von 1997 bis 1999 die *edition minotaurus* und gemeinsam mit Jan Wagner gab er 2003 und 2008 die Anthologien *Lyrik von Jetzt* I und II heraus. Zuletzt gewann er 2013 den Kunstpreis Lotto Brandenburg.

Veröffentlichungen (Auswahl) / Publications (selected)
Es gibt hier keine Küstenstraßen. Gedichte (Lyrikedition 2001)
Am Ende kommen Touristen. Gedichte (Berlin Verlag 2002)
Großes Kino. Gedichte (Berlin Verlag 2005)
Von der Oberfläche der Erde. Gedichte (Berlin Verlag 2009)
Die Stille zwischen null und eins. Gedichte (Hanser Berlin 2013)
Wir sind jetzt hier – Neue Wanderungen durch die Mark Brandenburg (gemeinsam mit Tom Schulz) (Hanser Berlin 2014)
Großraumtaxi – Berliner Szenen (Verbrecher Verlag 2014)
Die Sprache von Gibraltar. Gedichte (Hanser Berlin 2016)

PETER MACKAY

Peter Mackay's (born 1979, Isle of Lewis) texts are influenced by the long and tumultuous history of his birthplace, in which the "names and nouns are relics and scorings of different cultures – Norse, Gaelic, Scottish, Anglo-Saxon". As such, he writes in Scottish-Gaelic as well as English, and links the traditions of the old languages and the myths and tropes that they transmit, with a present which is marked by constant breaks, a continual changing and remembering. Mackay has lived in Glasgow, Barcelona, Dublin and Edinburgh and currently works as a lecturer at the University of St. Andrews. In his academic work he has published diverse books on Gaelic, Scottish and Irish poetry and literature. He has translated poems from Spanish, Danish, French and Irish-Gaelic into English. Mackay was nominated for the "Donald Meek" and "Duais Colmchille" Prizes. His poems have been published in diverse magazines, and his book of poems *Bàta Taigh Bàta / Boat House Boat* is to be published by Acair Press in 2014.

PETER MACKAY

Die Gedichte von Peter Mackay (*1979 Isle of Lewis) sind von der langen und bewegten Geschichte seines Geburtsorts geprägt, in dem die »Namen und Nomen Reliquien und Besetzungen verschiedener Kulturen sind – altnordisch, gälisch, angelsächsisch«. So schreibt er sowohl auf Englisch als auch auf Schottisch-Gälisch und verknüpft die Tradition der alten Sprache und die durch sie übermittelten alten Mythen und Tropen mit einer Gegenwart, die sich durch ein konstantes Aufbrechen, ein stetiges sich Ändern und Erinnern auszeichnet. Mackay lebte in Glasgow, Barcelona, Dublin und Edinburgh und arbeitet derzeit als Dozent an der St. Andrews Universität. Er veröffentlichte diverse Bücher über gälische, schottische und irische Poesie und Literatur. Als Übersetzer überträgt er Gedichte aus dem Spanischen, Dänischen, Französischen und Irish-Gälischen ins Englische. Mackay wurde für den Donald-Meek-Preis und den Duais-Cholmchille-Preis nominiert. Seine Gedichte sind in diversen Magazinen veröffentlicht, sein Gedichtband *Bàta Taigh Bàta / Boat House Boat* erschien 2014 bei Acair Press.

Veröffentlichungen (Auswahl) / Publications (selected)
From Another Island (Clutag Press 2010)
Bàta Taigh Bàta / Boat House Boat (Acair 2014)

J. O. MORGAN

J. O. Morgan (born 1978 Edinburgh) lives on a small farm in The Scottish Borders. In 2009 he won the Aldeburgh First Poetry Prize with his book-length poem about a young boy named Rocky from the Isle of Skye. The lyrically treated biographical sketch *Natural Mechanical* excited the jury with its complex yet accessible handling of a personal history. Morgan's texts move between truth and fiction, tradition and individual perspective, and distinguish themselves through a dexterous use of various verse forms. Following *Natural Mechanical*, the poetry collection *Long Cuts* was published in 2012, and was nominated for the "Scottish Book Award", and in 2014 the disturbing reworking of the Anglo-saxon text about the Battle of Maldon in 991 AD *At Maldon* appeared.

J. O. MORGAN

J. O. Morgan (*1978 Edinburgh) lebt auf einer kleinen Farm in den Scottish Borders. 2009 gewann er mit seinem ersten Gedichtband über den jungen Rocky von der Insel Skye den Aldeburgh First Poetry Preis. Der lyrisch verarbeitete biographische Sketch *Natural Mechanical* begeisterte die Jury durch seinen komplexen und doch extrem zugänglichen Umgang mit einer persönlichen Geschichte. Morgans Texte bewegen sich zwischen Wahrheit und Fiktion, Tradition und individueller Perspektive und zeichnen sich durch einen gewandten Umgang mit unterschiedlichen Versformen aus. Auf *Natural Mechanical* folgte 2012 die Gedichtsammlung *Long Cuts*, welche für den Scottish Book Award nominiert wurde, und 2014 *At Maldon*, die verstörende

Aktualisierung des angelsächsischen Textes über die Schlacht von Maldon 991 n. Chr.

Veröffentlichungen (Auswahl) / Publications (selected)
Natural Mechanical (CB Editions 2009)
Long Cuts (CB Editions 2012)
At Maldon (CB Editions 2014)

DON PATERSON

Don Paterson, born in Dundee, Scotland, in 1963, is thought of as one of the greatest poetic talents of his generation. A master of classical forms and poet of everyday things, Paterson's poetry is in the tradition of Scottish poetry without being traditionalistic. Whether he writes about the death of a pet, morphine boxes lying around or the felling of an old tree, there's always more at stake in a Paterson poem. One could even say everything is at stake. The *Independent* wrote of him that he is "one of the few contemporary poets whose work combines postmodern playfulness with a feel for the yearning for transcendence." His preoccupation with poetry has always run parallel to his preoccupation with music. In 1984 Paterson moved to London to work as a jazz musician and started writing poems at about the same time. During the 90s he lived between England and Scotland and between art forms. He wrote and played music, wrote columns on painting and reviewed video games for the *Times*. Even now he works in several genres, writing aphorisms and plays for stage and radio as well as poems and continuing to compose music. He is the poetry editor for the renowned Picador publishing house and Professor of Poetry at the University of St Andrews. He has published six volumes of poetry since 1993 and won many prizes, being the first poet to win the T. S. Eliot Prize twice. He was made an OBE in 2008.

DON PATERSON

Don Paterson (*1963 Dundee, Schottland) ist Meister klassischer Formen, Dichter alltäglicher Dinge. Der Tod eines Haustiers, herumliegende Morphiumschachteln oder das Fällen eines alten Baums – es geht ums Konkrete und zugleich um mehr in Patersons Lyrik. Die Beschäftigung mit Literatur lief immer parallel zur Beschäftigung mit Musik: 1984 zog Paterson nach London, um als Jazzmusiker zu arbeiten, und begann zur gleichen Zeit, Gedichte zu verfassen. In den 90er Jahren pendelte er zwischen England und Schottland und zwischen den Künsten: Er spielte Musik und komponierte, schrieb Kolumnen zur Malerei und rezensierte Videospiele für die *Times*. Auch heute arbeitet er genre-übergreifend, neben Gedichten verfasst er Aphorismen, Theaterstücke und Hörspiele, komponiert weiterhin Musik, ist Herausgeber des Lyrikprogramms beim renommierten Verlagshaus Picador und Professor für Dichtung an der University of St Andrews. Seit 1993 sind sechs Gedichtbände von ihm erschienen, für die er zahlreiche Preise erhielt. So ist Paterson ist u. a. der erste Dichter, der zweimal den T. S. Eliot Award verliehen bekam. 2008 wurde er zum Officer of the Order of the British Empire ernannt.

Veröffentlichungen (Auswahl) / Publications (selected)
Nil Nil (Faber 1993)
God's Gift to Women (Faber 1997)
White Lie. Selected Poems (Graywolf 2001)
Landing Light (Faber 2003)
Orpheus – after Rilke's Die Sonette an Orpheus (Faber 2006)
Rain (Faber 2009)

Veröffentlichungen in deutscher Übersetzung / Publications in german translation
Kerzenvogel. Aus dem Englischen von Henning Ahrens (Luchterhand 2006)
Weiß wie der Mond. Aus dem Englischen von Henning Ahrens (Luchterhand 2007)

ROBIN ROBERTSON

Robin Robertson's (born 1955, Scone/Perthshire) poems have their roots in the rich tradition of Greek myths and Celtic folklore. They evoke, in forceful and melodious language, the arresting landscape and nature of North East Scotland. In 1997, Robertson's book of poems *A Painted Field* won the Forward Prize for Best First Collection. For this publication, he also received the Adleburgh Poetry Festival Prize and the Saltire Scottish First Book of the Year Prize. The book was also one of the Sunday Times Books of the Year. As a publisher, Robertson is also an institution in British literature. Among others, he has brought out works by Anne Carson, J. M. Coetzee, Seamus Deane, Geoffrey Hill, Michael Longley and Sharon Olds. Hanser Verlag recently published a selection of his work under the title *Am Robbenkap*, in Jan Wagner's translations. *Sailing the Forest* – his selected poems in English – is now out with Picador and Farrar, Straus and Giroux.

ROBIN ROBERTSON

Die Gedichte Robin Robertsons (*1955 Scone/Perthshire) wurzeln in der reichen Tradition griechischer Mythen und keltischer Folklore. Sie evozieren in kraftvoller und melodiöser Sprache die eindrucksvolle Landschaft und Natur des nordöstlichen Schottlands. Bereits 1997 gewann Robertsons Gedichtband *A Painted Field* den Forward Prize für das beste Debüt. Für diese Veröffentlichung erhielt er außerdem den Aldeburgh-Poetry-Festival-Preis und den Saltire-Scottish-First-Book-of-the-Year Preis. Das Buch wurde zudem von der Sunday Times ausgezeichnet. Robertson ist auch als Verleger eine Institution der britischen Literatur. Unter anderem gab er Werke von Anne Carson, J. M. Coetzee, Seamus Deane, Geoffrey Hill, Michael Longley und Sharon Olds heraus. Seine ausgewählten Gedichte erschienen 2014 im Band *Sailing the Forest* bei FGS und Picador.

Veröffentlichungen (Auswahl) / Publications (selected)
A Painted Field (Picador 1997)
Slow Air (Picador 2002)
Swithering (Picador 2006)

Tranströmer, The Deleted World (Enitharmon, 2006)
Euripides, Medea (Vintage 2008)
The Wrecking Light (Picador 2010)
Hill of Doors (Picador 2013)
Euripides, Bacchae (Vintage 2014)

Veröffentlichung in deutscher Übersetzung / Publication in german translation
Am Robbenkap. Gedichte. Aus dem Englischen von Jan Wagner (Edition Lyrik Kabinett
bei Hanser 2013)

KATHARINA SCHULTENS

In 2013, Katharina Schultens (born 1980, Kirchen/Sieg) was awarded the Leonce-und-
Lena Prize for the "courageous and innovative way" in which she "takes a core piece
of the contemporary world into consideration, and into language: the subject thrown
under the wheels of the financial system". Schulten's poems continually permeate
specialised languages, which she represents by weaving them into new complexity.
Thus the poet takes on biology or corporate finance and speculation in her last book of
poems, *gorgos portfolio* which moves from the figure of Medusa in Greek Mythology to
the contemporary working conditions of women. Schultens has been working at the
Humboldt University since 2006, becoming the Manager of the School of Analytical
Sciences Adlershof there in 2012, studied Cultural Studies in Hildesheim, St Louis and
Bologna. Since 1998 she has been publishing her poetry in magazines and anthologies.
In 2014, she won second prize in the "lauter niemand" prize for political poetry IV.

KATHARINA SCHULTENS

2013 wurde Katharina Schultens (*1980 Kirchen/Sieg) der Leonce-und-Lena-Preis
für die »mutige und innovative Weise« verliehen, in der sie »ein Kernstück der
zeitgenössischen Welt in Blick und Sprache nimmt: das unter das System der
Wirtschaft gekippte Subjekt«. Immer wieder durchdringen Schultens Gedichte
Fachsprachen, die sie in neuer Komplexität vernetzt und darstellt. So beschäftigt sich
die Lyrikerin mit Biologie oder Finanzwirtschaft und Spekulation und geht z. B. in
ihrem letzten Gedichtband *gorgos portfolio* über die Medusenfigur der griechischen
Mythologie auf gegenwärtige weibliche Arbeitsbedingungen ein.
Schultens, die seit 2006 an der Humboldt-Universität arbeitet und dort 2012
Geschäftsführerin der School of Analytical Sciences Adlershof wurde, studierte
Kulturwissenschaften in Hildesheim, St Louis und Bologna. Seit 1998 erscheint
ihre Lyrik und Poesie in Zeitschriften und Anthologien. In 2014 wurde sie zweite
Preisträgerin des lauter niemand-Preis für politische Lyrik IV.

Veröffentlichungen (Auswahl) / Publications (selected)
Aufbrüche. Gedichte (Rhein-Mosel-Verlag 2004)
gierstabil. Gedichte (Luxbooks 2011)
gorgos portfolio. Gedichte (kookbooks 2014)

RYAN VAN WINKLE

The poet Ryan Van Winkle (born 1977, New Haven), originally from Connecticut, USA, first arrived in Scotland for the turn of the millennium, and since then has made it his home. He is indefatigably active in the poetry scene there in various roles: as poet, literary promoter, journalist, as curator of the poetry space "The Forest", and more recently, as a performer. *Red like our room used to feel* was celebrated as one of the highlights of the Edinburgh Fringe Festival. Van Winkle's texts are the expression of a stark, often uneasy emotional honesty. In one performance project, for example, he gave individual readings to his audience in a space that recreated his own bedroom. Van Winkle was the first Reader in Residence of the Scottish Poetry Library and is currently Poet in Residence of the Edinburgh City Libraries. His first book of poetry, *Tomorrow, We'll Live Here* won the 2009 Crashaw Prize for a First Publication.

RYAN VAN WINKLE

Der ursprünglich aus Connecticut, USA, stammende Dichter Ryan Van Winkle (*1977 New Haven) kam zur Jahrtausendwende das erste Mal nach Schottland und betrachtet die Region seither als seine Heimat. In der dortigen Poesieszene ist er unermüdlich und auf vielen Bühnen unterwegs: als Dichter, Literaturvermittler, Journalist, als Kurator des Poesieraumes »The Forest« und neuerdings auch als Performer. *Red like our room used to feel* wurde 2012 als eines der Highlights des Edinburgh Fringe Festivals gefeiert. Van Winkles Texte sind Ausdruck einer starken, oft unbehaglichen emotionalen Ehrlichkeit. So auch ein Performanceprojekt, in dem er seinem Publikum in einem dem eigenen Zimmer nachempfundenen Raum Einzellesungen gab. Van Winkle war der erste Reader in Residence der Scottish Poetry Library und ist derzeit Poet in Residence der Edinburgh City Libraries. Sein erster Gedichtband *Tomorrow, We'll Live Here* gewann 2009 den Crashaw-Preis für Erstpublikationen.

Veröffentlichungen (Auswahl) / Publications (selected)

Tomorrow, We'll Live Here (Salt Publications 2010)
ViewMaster (Stewed Rhubarb 2014)
The Good Dark (Penned in the Margins 2015)

Aurélie Maurin wurde 1975 in Paris geboren und hat Literaturwissenschaft und Linguistik in Paris studiert. Sie lebt seit 2000 als freie Literaturübersetzerin, Kuratorin und Veranstalterin für verschiedene Institutionen in Berlin (u.a. Literaturwerkstatt Berlin, Haus der Kulturen der Welt). Sie ist Herausgeberin der Buchreihe VERS-schmuggel beim Verlag das Wunderhorn und der deutsch-französischen Kunst- und Literaturzeitschrift La mer gelée.

Aurélie Maurin was born in Paris in 1975, and studied literature and linguistics in Paris. Since 2000, she has lived in Berlin, where she works as a literary translator, and as a curator and event organiser for various institutions (among others, Literaturwerkstatt Berlin and Haus der Kulturen der Welt). She is editor of the VERS-schmuggel series (Verlag das Wunderhorn), and of the German-French art and literature magazine La mer gelée.

Dr. Thomas Wohlfahrt ist Gründungsdirektor der Literaturwerkstatt Berlin und leitet sie seit 1991. Der promovierte Literatur- und Musikwissenschaftler initiierte und leitete internationale Großprojekte wie den Literatur Express Europa 2000, die Webseite lyrikline.org, das ZEBRA Poetry Film Festival, den open mike und das poesie-festival berlin. Er ist Mitglied zahlreicher nationaler wie internationaler Gremien und kuratiert und berät verschiedene internationale Literatur- und Kunstprogramme.

Thomas Wohlfahrt is the founding director of the Literaturwerkstatt Berlin. He has been in charge since 1991. A doctor of literature and music, he has initiated and directed major international projects such as Literature Express Europe 2000, the lyrikline.org website and the poesiefestival berlin. Wohlfahrt is a member of many national and international organisations and is curator and adviser for various international literature and art programmes

ANNA CROWE
»A Calender of Hares«, »Sari«
Aus: *Punk with Dulcimer* (Peterloo 2006)

MICHAEL DONHAUSER
»Vielleicht regnet es«
Aus: *Ich habe lange nicht doch nur an dich gedacht* (Matthes & Seitz)
»Es gab, da war der Mond«
Aus: *Variationen in Prosa, Variationen im März* (Matthes & Seitz 2013)

ULRIKE DRAESNER
»schöneweide schöneweide«
Aus: *subsong.* Gedichte (Luchterhand 2014)

ODILE KENNEL
»Tiere zu fragen«
Aus: *oder wie heißt diese interplanetare Luft* (dtv 2013)

ROBIN ROBERTSON
Aus: *Sailing the Forest* (Picador/Farrar, Straus & Giroux 2014)

Dieses Buch kam zustande mit freundlicher Unterstützung durch /
With the generous support of:

Lektorat / Text-editing: Odile Kennel, Aurélie Maurin, Charlotte Thiessen

Übersetzungen / Translations
Vorwort / Preface: Isabel Cole. Statements : Sam Langer, Charlotte Thiessen

© 2015 Verlag Das Wunderhorn, Rohrbacher Straße 18,
   D-69115 Heidelberg www.wunderhorn.de
© 2015 Freight Books, 49 Virginia Street,
   Glasgow G1 1TS, Schottland www.freightbooks.co.uk
© für die Übersetzungen bei den Autorinnen und Autoren
   for the translations is held by the authors / translators

Gestaltung / Design: Cornelia Feyll und Friedrich Forssman, Kassel
Herstellung / Production: Cyan, Heidelberg
Druck / Printing: NINO Druck GmbH, Neustadt/Weinstraße
ISBN 9783884235034 (Deutschland) ISBN 9781910449752 (Schottland)

Leichte Abweichungen zwischen Gehörtem und Geschriebenem liegen in
den Nachbereitungen der Übersetzungen begründet.
Slight variations between the audio and written text are a result of the
reworking of the translations.